The Maths Teachers' Handbook

Jane Portman and
Jeremy Richardson

Heinemann  VSO

Heinemann Educational Publishers
Halley Court, Jordan Hill, Oxford OX2 8EJ
A division of Reed Educational & Professional Publishing Ltd

Heinemann Educational Books (Nigeria) Ltd
PMB 5205, Ibadan
Heinemann Educational Botswana (Publishers) (Pty) Ltd
PO Box 10103, Village Post Office, Gaborone, Botswana

FLORENCE PRAGUE MADRID ATHENS
MELBOURNE AUCKLAND TOKYO SINGAPORE
PORTSMOUTH (NH) MEXICO CHICAGO SAO PAULO
JOHANNESBURG KAMPALA NAIROBI

Voluntary Service Overseas
317 Putney Bridge Road, London
© VSO 1997

First published by Heinemann Educational Publishers in 1997

British Library Cataloguing in Publication Data
A catalogue record for this book is available from the British Library

Cover design by Threefold and Susan Clarke
Cover illustration by Pat Murray
Textual illustrations by Pat Murray and John Gilkes

ISBN 0 435 92318 8

Designed by Susan Clarke
Phototypeset by Roger Stevens
Printed and bound in Great Britain
by The Bath Press

97 98 99 10 9 8 7 6 5 4 3 2 1

Contents

Acknowledgements

Many people have contributed ideas and information to this text. In particular, the authors would like to thank:
ATM Bilingual students and Mathematics Working Group; SMILE; NIAS Mathematics team; their co-tutors on the VSO Maths/Science courses; the VSO volunteers on the VSO Maths/Science courses; and Silke Bernau, Penny Amerena and Janet Orlek for their patience and editing skills.

The authors are grateful to the following for permission to reproduce illustrations:
Phil Dodd, who has extensively researched mathematical topics of a multicultural background, for permission to reproduce illustrations of the Arabic number square, Egyptian numbers, Designing Rangoli patterns, Islamic pattern, The symmetry of Islamic patterns, Designing your own Islamic patterns, The Sri Jantra, Cows and leopards and Hausa numbers from books he has written on this topic specifically for classroom use. *Mathematics from Around the World* and *Global Mathematics* can be obtained from Phil Dodd at 73 Beech Grove, Whitley Bay, Tyne and Wear, NE26 3PL, UK; SMILE for permission to reproduce 'Which Numbers' from SMILE Card 1786; ATM for permission to reproduce the illustration at the top of page 80: 'Considering language' from *Talking Maths, Talking Languages*; NIAS for permission to reproduce the Glossary.

Introduction

Who is this book for?

This book is for mathematics teachers working in higher primary and secondary schools in developing countries. The book will help teachers improve the quality of mathematical education because it deals specifically with some of the challenges which many maths teachers in the developing world face, such as a lack of ready-made teaching aids, possible textbook shortages, and teaching and learning maths in a second language.

Why has this book been written?

Teachers all over the world have developed different ways to teach maths successfully in order to raise standards of achievement. Maths teachers have

- developed ways of using locally available resources
- adapted mathematics to their own cultural contexts and to the tasks and problems in their own communities
- introduced local maths-related activities into their classrooms
- improved students' understanding of English in the maths classroom.

This book brings together many of these tried and tested ideas from teachers worldwide, including the extensive experience of VSO maths teachers and their national colleagues working together in schools throughout Africa, Asia, the Caribbean and the Pacific.

We hope teachers everywhere will use the ideas in this book to help students increase their mathematical knowledge and skills.

How can I get all my students to do better in their maths exam?

I can demonstrate some mathematical ideas with string, matchboxes and bottle tops.

I want to show students how ancient Egyptians used many of the mathematical ideas in the textbook.

Students need to see how mathematics is part of their daily lives. It is not only a school activity.

I want to introduce this topic in geometry with some hands-on practical activities.

What are the aims of this book?

This book will help maths teachers:
- find new and successful ways of teaching maths
- make maths more interesting and more relevant to their students
- understand some of the language and cultural issues their students experience.

Most of all, we hope this book will contribute to improving the quality of mathematics education and to raising standards of achievement.

What are the main themes of this book?

There are four main issues in the teaching and learning of mathematics:

Teaching methods

Students learn best when the teacher uses a wide range of teaching methods. This book gives examples and ideas for using many different methods in the classroom.

Resources and teaching aids

Students learn best by doing things: constructing, touching, moving, investigating. There are many ways of using cheap and available resources in the classroom so that students can learn by doing. This book shows how to teach a lot using very few resources such as bottle tops, string, matchboxes.

The language of the learner

Language is as important as mathematics in the mathematics classroom. In addition, learning in a second language causes special difficulties. This book suggests activities to help students use language to improve their understanding of maths.

The culture of the learner

Students do all sorts of maths at home and in their communities. This is often very different from the maths they do in school. This book provides activities which link these two types of maths together. Examples are taken from all over the world. Helping students make this link will improve their mathematics.

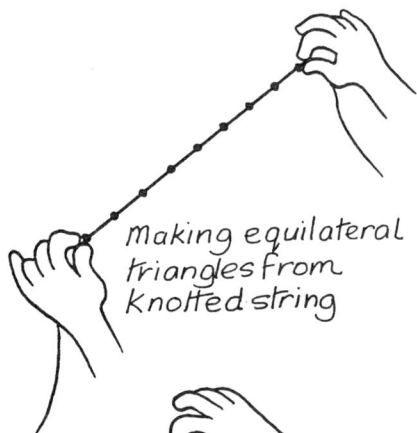

making equilateral triangles from knotted string

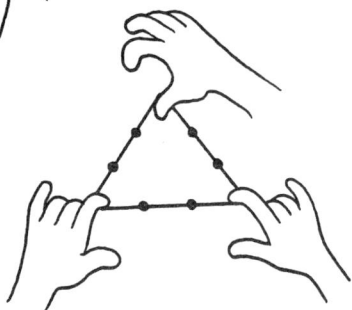

Making shapes from matchboxes

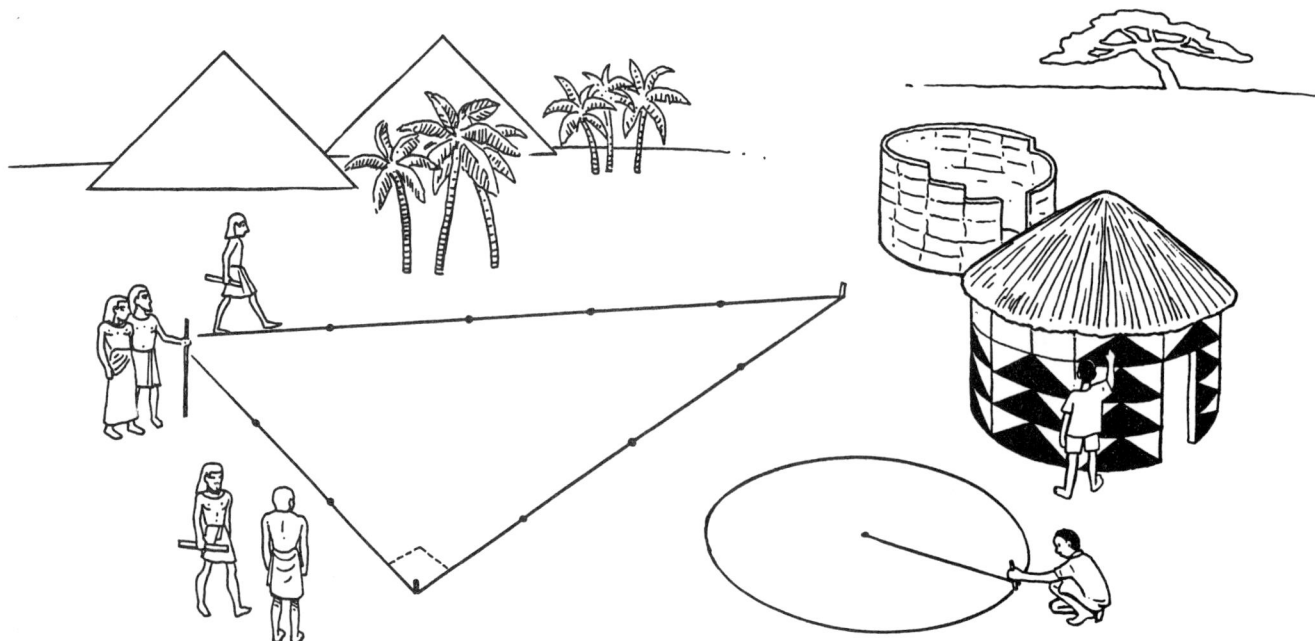

How did we select the activities and teaching ideas in this book?

There are over 100 different activities in this book which teachers can use to help vary their teaching methods and to promote students' understanding of maths.

The activities have been carefully chosen to show a range of different teaching methods, which need few teaching aids. The activities cover a wide range of mathematical topics.

Each activity:
- shows the mathematics to be learned
- contains clear instructions for students
- introduces interesting ways for students to learn actively.

What is mathematics?

Mathematics is a way of organising our experience of the world. It enriches our understanding and enables us to communicate and make sense of our experiences. It also gives us enjoyment. By doing mathematics we can solve a range of practical tasks and real-life problems. We use it in many areas of our lives.

In mathematics we use ordinary language and the special language of mathematics. We need to teach students to use both these languages.

We can work on problems within mathematics and we can work on problems that use mathematics as a tool, like problems in science and geography. Mathematics can describe and explain but it can also predict what might happen. That is why mathematics is important.

Learning and teaching mathematics

Learning skills and remembering facts in mathematics are important but they are only the means to an end. Facts and skills are not important in themselves. They are important when we need them to solve a problem. Students will remember facts and skills easily when they use them to solve real problems.

As well as using mathematics to solve real-life problems, students should also be taught about the different parts of mathematics, and how they fit together.

Mathematics can be taught using a step-by-step approach to a topic but it is important to show that many topics are linked, as shown in the diagram on the next page.

It is also important to show students that mathematics is done all over the world.

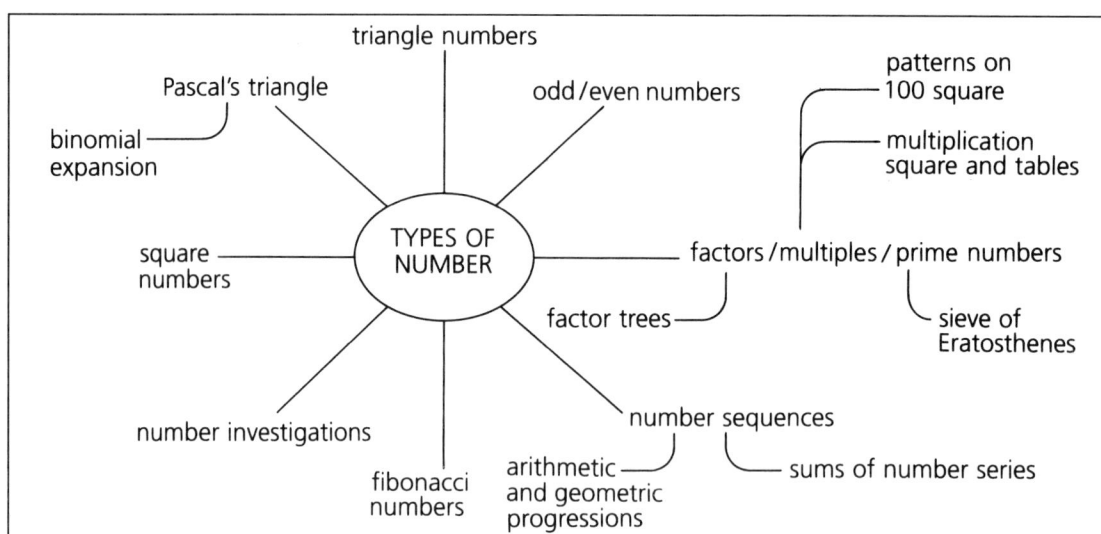

Although each country may have a different syllabus, there are many topics that are taught all over the world. Some of these are:

- number systems and place value
- arithmetic
- algebra
- geometry
- statistics
- trigonometry
- probability
- graphs
- measurement

We can show students how different countries have developed different maths to deal with these topics.

How to use this book

This book is not simply a collection of teaching ideas and activities. It describes an approach to teaching and learning mathematics.

This book can be best used as part of an approach to teaching using a plan or scheme of work to guide your teaching. This book is only one resource out of several that can be used to help you with ideas for activities and teaching methods to meet the needs of all pupils and to raise standards of achievement.

There are three ways of using this book:

Planning a topic

Use your syllabus to decide which topic you are going to teach next. Find that topic in the index at the back of the book. Turn to the relevant pages and select activities that are suitable. We suggest that you try the activities yourself before you use them in the classroom. You might like to discuss them with a colleague or try out the activity on a small group of students. Then think about how you can or need to adapt and improve the activity for students of different abilities and ages.

Improving your own teaching

One way to improve your own teaching is to try new methods and activities in the classroom and then think about how well the activity improved students' learning. Through trying out new activities and working in different ways, and then reflecting on the lesson and analysing how well students have learned, you can develop the best methods for your students.

You can decide to concentrate on one aspect of teaching maths: language, culture, teaching methods, resources or planning. Find the relevant chapter and use it.

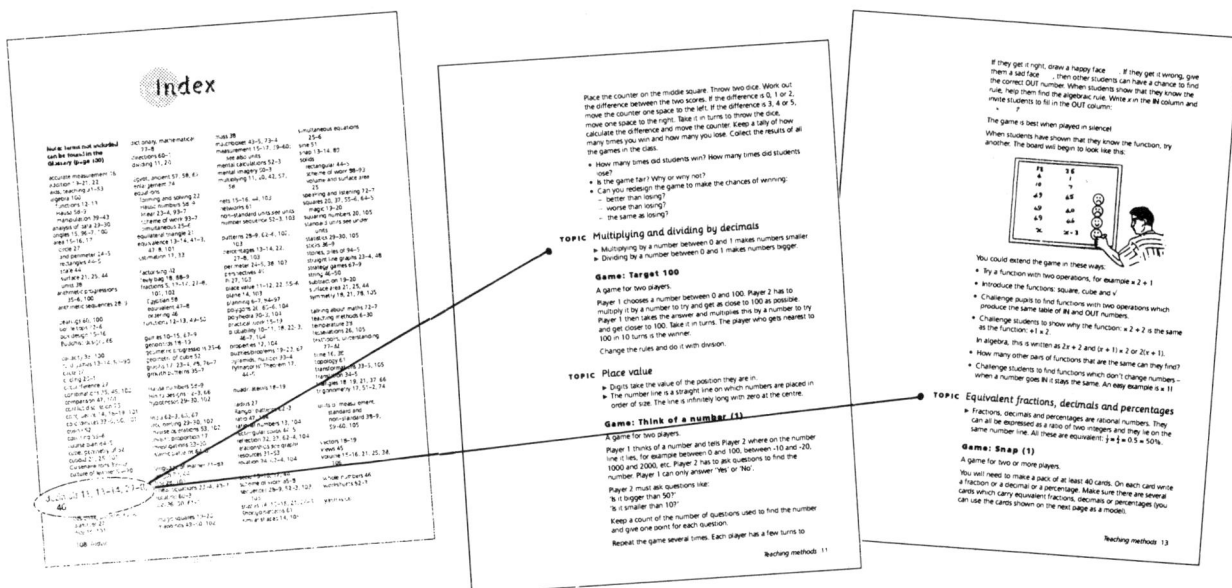

Working with colleagues

Each chapter can be used as material for a workshop with colleagues. There is material for workshops on:
• developing different teaching methods
• developing resources and teaching aids
• culture in the maths classroom
• language in the maths classroom
• planning schemes of work.

In the workshops, teachers can try out activities and discuss the issues raised in the chapter. You can build up a collection of successful activities and add to it as you make up your own, individually or with other teachers.

CHAPTER 1 Teaching methods

This chapter is about the different ways you can teach a topic in the classroom. Young people learn things in many different ways. They don't always learn best by sitting and listening to the teacher. Students can learn by:
- practising skills on their own
- discussing mathematics with each other
- playing mathematical games
- doing puzzles
- doing practical work
- solving problems
- finding things out for themselves.

In the classroom, students need opportunities to use different ways of learning. Using a range of different ways of learning has the following benefits:
- it motivates students
- it improves their learning skills
- it provides variety
- it enables them to learn things more quickly.

We will look at the following teaching methods:
1 Presentation and explanation by the teacher
2 Consolidation and practice
3 Games
4 Practical work
5 Problems and puzzles
6 Investigating mathematics

Presentation and explanation by the teacher

This is a formal teaching method which involves the teacher presenting and explaining mathematics to the whole class. It can be difficult because you have to ensure that all students understand. This can be a very effective way of:
- teaching a new piece of mathematics to a large group of students
- drawing together everyone's understanding at certain stages of a topic
- summarising what has been learnt.

Planning content before the lesson:

- Plan the content to be taught. Check up any points you are not sure of. Decide how much content you will cover in the session.

- Identify the key points and organise them in a logical order. Decide which points you will present first, second, third and so on.
- Choose examples to illustrate each key point.
- Prepare visual aids in advance.
- Organise your notes in the order you will use them. Cards can be useful, one for each key point and an example.

Planning and organising time

- Plan carefully how to pace each lesson. How much time will you give to your presentation and explanation of mathematics? How much time will you leave for questions and answers by students? How much time will you allow for students to practise new mathematics, to do different activities like puzzles, investigations, problems and so on?
- With careful planning and clear explanations, you will find that you do not need to talk for too long. This will give students time to do mathematics themselves, rather than sitting and listening to you doing the work.

You need to organise time:
- to introduce new ideas
- for students to complete the task set
- for students to ask questions
- to help students understand
- to set and go over homework
- for practical equipment to be set up and put away
- for students to move into and out of groups for different activities.

Organising the classroom

- Organise the classroom so that all students will be able to see you when you are talking.
- Clean the chalkboard. If necessary, prepare notes on the chalkboard in advance to save time in the lesson.
- Arrange the teacher's table so that it does not restrict your movement at the front of the class. Place the table in a position which does not create a barrier between you and the students.
- Organise the tables and chairs for students according to the type of activity:
  - facing the chalkboard if the teacher is talking to the whole group
  - in circles for group work.
- Develop a routine for the beginning of each lesson so that all students know what behaviour is expected of them from the beginning of the session. For example, begin by going over homework.
- Create a pleasant physical environment. For example, display students' work and teaching resources – create a 'puzzle corner'.

Performance

- It is very important that your voice is clear and loud enough for all students to hear.
- Vary the pitch and tone of your voice.
- Ask students questions at different stages of the lesson to check they have understood the content so far. Ask questions which will make them think and develop their understanding as well as show you that they heard what you said.
- For new classes, learn the names of students as quickly as possible.
- Use students' names when questioning.
- Speak with conviction. If you sound hesitant you may lose students' confidence in you.
- When using the chalkboard, plan carefully where you write things. It helps to divide the board into sections and work through each section systematically.
- Try not to end a lesson in the middle of a teaching point or example.
- Plan a clear ending to the session.

Ground rules for classroom behaviour

- Students need to know what behaviour is acceptable and unacceptable in the classroom.
- Establish a set of ground rules with students. Display the rules in the classroom.
- Start simply with a small number of rules of acceptable behaviour. For example, rules about entering and leaving the room and rules about starting and finishing lessons on time.
- Identify acceptable behaviour in the following situations:
  - when students need help
  - when students need resources
  - when students have forgotten to bring books or homework to the lesson
  - when students find the work too easy or too hard.

Consolidation and practice

It is very important that students have the opportunity to practise new mathematics and to develop their understanding by applying new ideas and skills to new problems and new contexts.

The main source of exercises for consolidation and practice is the text book.

It is important to check that the examples in the exercises are graded from easy to difficult and that students don't start with the hardest examples. It is also important to ensure that what is being practised is actually the topic that has been covered and not new content or a new skill which has not been taught before.

This is a very common teaching method. You should take care that you do not use it too often at the expense of other methods.

Select carefully which problems and which examples students should do from the exercises in the text book. Students can do and check practice exercises in a variety of ways. For example:

- Half the class can do all the odd numbers. The other half can do the even numbers. Then, in groups, students can check their answers and, if necessary, do corrections. Any problems that cannot be solved or agreed on can be given to another group as a challenge.
- Where classes are very large, teachers can mark a selection of the exercises, e.g. all odd numbers, or those examples that are most important for all students to do correctly.
- To check homework, select a few examples that need to be checked. Invite a different student to do each example on the chalkboard and explain it to the class. Make sure you choose students who did the examples correctly at home. Over time, try to give as many students as possible a chance to teach the class.

Homework – simple linear equations

① $3x - 7 = 14$
$3x$

③ $2y + 7 = 0$
$2y = -7$
y

⑤ $\frac{3x}{2} = 4$

$3x = 4 \times 2$

You can set time limits on students in order to help them work more quickly and increase the pace of their learning.

- When practising new mathematics, students should not have to do arithmetic that is harder than the new mathematics. If the arithmetic is harder than the new mathematics, students will get stuck on the arithmetic and they will not get to practise the new mathematics. Both the examples below ask students to practise finding the area of a rectangular field. But students will slow down or get stuck with the arithmetic of the second example.

✓ Find the area of a rectangular field which is 10 m long and 6 m wide.

✗ Find the area of a rectangular field which is 7.63 m long and 4.029 m wide.

- Questions must be easy to understand so that the skill can be practised quickly.

Both the examples below ask the same question. Students will understand the first example and practise finding the area of a circle. In the second example they will spend more time understanding the question than practising finding the area.

✓ A circular plate has a radius of 10 cm. Find its area.

✗ Find the area of the circular base of an electrical reading lamp. The base has a diameter of 30 cm.

· ·

Games

Using games can make mathematics classes very enjoyable, exciting and interesting. Mathematical games provide opportunities for students to be actively involved in learning. Games allow students to experience success and satisfaction, thereby building their enthusiasm and self-confidence.

But mathematical games are not simply about fun and confidence building. Games help students to:
- understand mathematical concepts
- develop mathematical skills
- know mathematical facts
- learn the language and vocabulary of mathematics
- develop ability in mental mathematics.

TOPIC Probability

▶ Probability is a measure of how likely an event is to happen.
▶ The more often an experiment is repeated, the closer the outcomes get to the theoretical probability.

Game: Left and right

You will need:
- *a counter e.g. a stone, a bottle top*
- *two dice*
- *a board with 7 squares*

A game for two players.

Make a board as shown.

counter

Place the counter on the middle square. Throw two dice. Work out the difference between the two scores. If the difference is 0, 1 or 2, move the counter one space to the left. If the difference is 3, 4 or 5, move one space to the right. Take it in turns to throw the dice, calculate the difference and move the counter. Keep a tally of how many times you win and how many you lose. Collect the results of all the games in the class.

- How many times did students win? How many times did students lose?
- Is the game fair? Why or why not?
- Can you redesign the game to make the chances of winning:
    - better than losing?
    - worse than losing?
    - the same as losing?

TOPIC Multiplying and dividing by decimals

▶ Multiplying by a number between 0 and 1 makes numbers smaller.
▶ Dividing by a number between 0 and 1 makes numbers bigger.

Game: Target 100

A game for two players.

Player 1 chooses a number between 0 and 100. Player 2 has to multiply it by a number to try and get as close to 100 as possible. Player 1 then takes the answer and multiplies this by a number to try and get closer to 100. Take it in turns. The player who gets nearest to 100 in 10 turns is the winner.

Change the rules and do it with division.

TOPIC Place value

▶ Digits take the value of the position they are in.
▶ The number line is a straight line on which numbers are placed in order of size. The line is infinitely long with zero at the centre.

Game: Think of a number (1)

A game for two players.

Player 1 thinks of a number and tells Player 2 where on the number line it lies, for example between 0 and 100, between -10 and -20, 1000 and 2000, etc. Player 2 has to ask questions to find the number. Player 1 can only answer 'Yes' or 'No'.

Player 2 must ask questions like:
'Is it bigger than 50?'
'Is it smaller than 10?'

Keep a count of the number of questions used to find the number and give one point for each question.

Repeat the game several times. Each player has a few turns to choose a number and a few turns to ask questions and find the number. The player with the fewest points wins.

TOPIC Properties of numbers

▶ Numbers can be classified and identified by their properties e.g. odd/even, factors, multiple, prime, rectangular, square, triangular.

Game: Think of a number (2)

A game for two players.

Player 1 thinks of a number between 0 and 100. Player 2 has to find the number Player 1 is thinking of. Player 2 asks Player 1 questions about the properties of the number, for example
'Is it a prime number?'
'Is it a square number?'
'Is it a triangular number?'
'Is it an odd number?'
'Is it a multiple of 3?'
'Is it a factor of 10?'

Player 1 can only answer 'Yes' or 'No'.

Player 2 will find it helpful to have a 10 × 10 numbered square to cross off the numbers as they work.

Each player has a few turns to choose a number and a few turns to ask questions and find the number.

TOPIC Algebraic functions

▶ A function is a rule connecting every member of a set of numbers to a unique number in a different set, for example $x \rightarrow 3x$, $x \rightarrow 2x + 1$

Game: Discover the function

A game for the whole class.

Think of a simple function, for example × 3

Write a number on the left of the chalkboard. This will be an IN number, though it is important not to tell students at this stage. Opposite your number, write the OUT number. For example:
     10   30

Show two more lines. Choose any numbers and apply the function rule × 3:
     5   15
     7   21

Now write an IN number only and invite a student to come to the board to write the OUT number:
     11   ?

Discover the Function

If they get it right, draw a happy face ☺ . If they get it wrong, give them a sad face ☹ , then other students can have a chance to find the correct OUT number. When students show that they know the rule, help them find the algebraic rule. Write x in the IN column and invite students to fill in the OUT column:

x ?

The game is best when played in silence!

When students have shown that they know the function, try another. The board will begin to look like this:

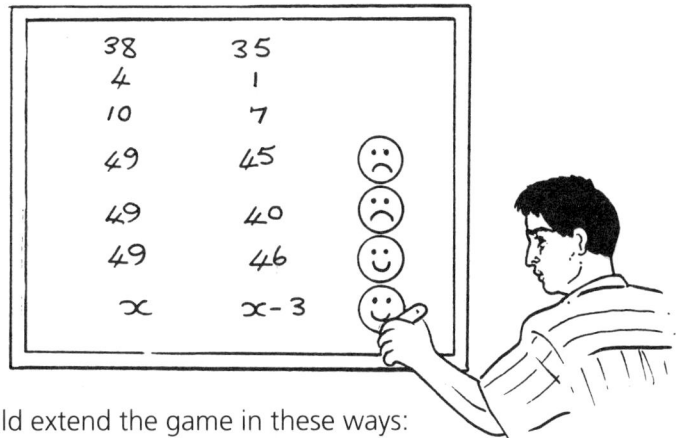

You could extend the game in these ways:

- Try a function with two operations, for example $\times 2 + 1$

- Introduce the functions: square, cube and $\sqrt{}$

- Challenge pupils to find functions with two operations which produce the same table of IN and OUT numbers.

- Challenge students to show why the function: $\times 2 + 2$ is the same as the function: $+1 \times 2$.

  In algebra, this is written as $2x + 2$ and $(x + 1) \times 2$ or $2(x + 1)$.

- How many other pairs of functions that are the same can they find?

- Challenge students to find functions which don't change numbers – when a number goes IN it stays the same. An easy example is $\times 1$!

TOPIC Equivalent fractions, decimals and percentages

▶ Fractions, decimals and percentages are rational numbers. They can all be expressed as a ratio of two integers and they lie on the same number line. All these are equivalent: $\frac{1}{2} = \frac{2}{4} = 0.5 = 50\%$.

Game: Snap (1)

A game for two or more players.

You will need to make a pack of at least 40 cards. On each card write a fraction or a decimal or a percentage. Make sure there are several cards which carry equivalent fractions, decimals or percentages (you can use the cards shown on the next page as a model).

$\frac{1}{2}$	$\frac{1}{4}$	$\frac{3}{4}$	$\frac{2}{4}$	$\frac{3}{12}$
0.75	25%	0.5	25%	10%
0.7	$\frac{10}{20}$	75%	20%	50%
0.2	0.1	0.8	$\frac{10}{50}$	$\frac{1}{10}$

Shuffle the cards and deal them out, face down, to the players. The players take it in turn to place one of their cards face up in the middle. The first player to see that a card is equivalent to another card face up in the middle must shout 'Snap!', and wins all the cards in the middle. The game continues until all the cards have been won. The winner is the player with the most cards.

TOPIC ## Similarity and congruence of shapes

- ▶ Plane shapes are similar when the corresponding sides are proportional and corresponding angles are equal.
- ▶ Plane shapes are similar if they are enlargements or reductions of each other.
- ▶ Plane shapes are congruent when they are exactly the same size and shape.

Game: Snap (2)

A game for two or more players.

You will need to make a pack of at least 20 cards with a shape on each card. Make a few pairs of cards with similar shapes and a few pairs of cards with congruent shapes. The game is played in the same way as Snap (1) above.

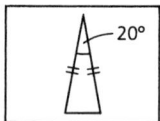

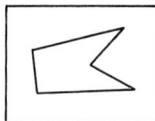

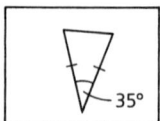

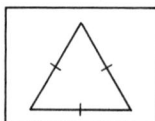

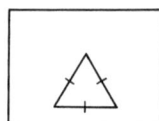

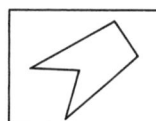

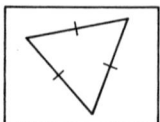

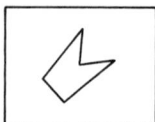

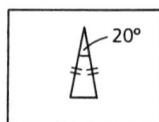

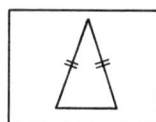

To win the pile of cards, the students must call out 'Similar' or 'Congruent' when the shapes on the top cards are similar or congruent.

TOPIC Estimating the size of angles

▶ Angle is a measure of turn. It is measured in degrees.
▶ Angles are acute (less than 90°), right angle (90°), obtuse (more than 90° and less than 180°) or reflex (more than 180°).

Game: Estimating an angle

Game for two players.

You will need:
• *a protractor*

Game A

Player 1 chooses an angle e.g. 49°. Player 2 has to draw that angle without using a protractor. Player 1 measures the angle with a protractor. Player 2 scores the number of points that is the difference between their angle size and the intended one. For example, Player 2's angle is measured to be 39°. So Player 2 scores 10 points (49°–39°).

Take it in turns. The winner is the player with the lowest score.

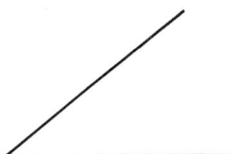

Player 2 tries to draw a 49° angle without a protractor

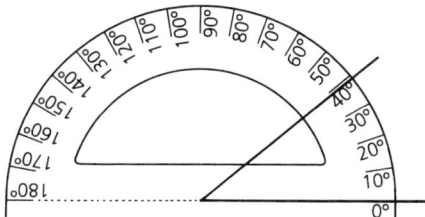

The angle measures 39°.
Player 2 scores 10 points (49°- 39°)

Game B

Each player draws 15 angles on a blank sheet of paper. They swap papers and estimate the size of each angle. Then they measure the angles with a protractor and compare the estimate and the exact measurement of the angles. Points are scored on the difference of the estimate and the actual size of each angle. The player with the lowest score wins.

Practical work

Practical work means three things:
• Using materials and resources to make things. This involves using mathematical skills of measuring and estimation and a knowledge of spatial relationships.
• Making a solid model of a mathematical concept or relationship.
• Using mathematics in a practical, real-life situation like in the marketplace, planning a trip, organising an event.

Practical work always involves using resources.

TOPICS Shapes, nets, area, volume, measurement, scale drawing

Activity: Design a box

A fruit seller wants to sell her fruit to shops in the next large town. She needs to transport the fruit safely and cheaply. She needs a box which can hold four pieces of fruit. The fruit must not roll about otherwise it will get damaged. The box must be strong enough so that it does not break when lifted.

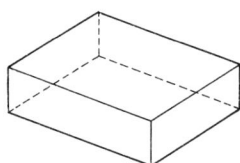

A box for bananas

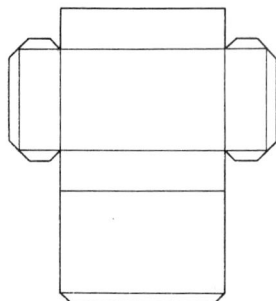

A net for the banana box

A box for oranges

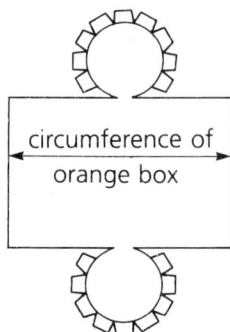

circumference of
orange box

Net for the box of oranges

In pairs, students can design a box which holds four pieces of fruit. Students need to make scale drawings of their design. Then four box designs can be compared and students can decide which design would be best for the fruit seller. Once the best design has been chosen, students may want to cut and make a few boxes from one piece of card. They can work from the scale drawing and test the design they chose.

To choose the best box design, students need to think about:

▶ **Shapes**
  • the strength of different box shapes
  • the shape that uses the least amount of card
  • the shape that packs best with other boxes of the same shape

▶ **Nets**
  • all the different nets for the shape of the box
  • where to put the tabs to glue the net together
  • how many nets for the box fit on one large piece of card without waste

▶ **Area**
  • surface area of shapes such as squares, rectangles, cylinders, triangles
  • total surface area of the net (including tabs)
  • which box shapes use the smallest amount of card

▶ **Volume**
  • the volume of boxes of different shapes
  • the smallest volume for their box shape so the fruit does not roll about

▶ **Measurement**
  • the size of the fruit in different arrangements
  • the arrangement that uses the least space
  • the accurate measurements for their chosen box shape

▶ **Scale drawing**
  • which scale to use
  • scaling down the accurate dimensions of the box, according to the scale factor
  • how to draw an accurate scale drawing of the box and its net

TOPICS *Accurate measurement, graphs and relationships*

Activity: 10 seconds

Design a pendulum to measure 10 seconds exactly. The pendulum must complete exactly 10 swings in 10 seconds. Experiment with different weights and lengths of string until the pendulum completes 10 swings in 10 seconds.

▶ Accurate measurement
  Students need to measure the mass of the weights, the time of 10 swings, length of the string etc.

You will need:
• *string*
• *drawing pins*
• *a ruler*
• *a watch*
• *some weights, for example stones*

▶ Graphs and relationships
Students need to decide what affects the length of time for 10 swings and how it affects it. For example, how does increasing or decreasing the length of string or the weight of the stone affect the time taken for 10 swings? To discover these relationships, students can draw graphs of the relationship between time and length of string or between time and weight.

TOPICS *Estimation, area, inverse proportion, scale drawings, Pythagoras' Theorem, trigonometry*

Activity: Shelter

Give students the following problem.

You and a friend are on a journey. It is nearly night time and you have nowhere to stay. You have a rectangular piece of cloth measuring 4 m by 3 m. Design a shelter to protect both of you from the wind and rain.

Decide:
• how much space you need to lie down
• what shape is best for your shelter
• what you will use to support the shelter – trees, rocks etc?

Help pupils by suggesting that they:
• begin by making scale drawings of possible shelters
• make a model of the shelter they choose
• estimate the heights and lengths of the shelter.

To solve the design problem, students need to:

▶ **Do estimations**
  • of the height of the people who will use the shelter
  • of the floor area of the shelter

▶ **Calculate area**
  • of the floor of different shelter designs such as rectangles, squares, regular and irregular polygons, triangles, circles

▶ **Understand inverse proportion**
  • for example, if the height of the shelter increases, the floor area decreases

▶ **Make scale drawings of different possible shelters**
  • based only on a few certain dimensions like length of one or two sides, radius

▶ **Use Pythagoras' Theorem and trigonometry**
  • to calculate the dimensions of the other parts of the shelter such as lengths of other sides and angles

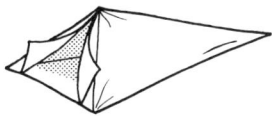

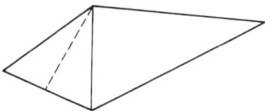

Isometric view of the shelter

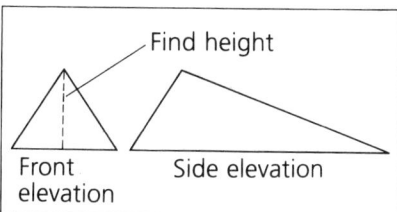

Scale drawing 1:50

TOPIC Probability

▶ different outcomes may occur when repeating the same experiment
▶ relative frequency can be used to estimate probabilities
▶ the greater the number of times an experiment is repeated, the closer the relative frequency gets to the theoretical probability.

Activity: Feely bag

Put different coloured beads in a bag, for example 5 red, 3 black and 1 yellow bead. Invite one student to take out a bead. The student should show the bead to the class and they should note its colour. The student then puts the bead back in the bag. Repeat over and over again, stop when students can say with confidence how many beads of each colour are in the bag.

Activity: The great race

You will need:
- *a grid for the race track, as shown*
- *2 dice*
- *a stone for each runner which can be moved along the race track*

Roll two dice and add up the two numbers to get a total. The runner whose number is the total can be moved forward one square. For example, [dice] + [dice] = 9, so runner 9 moves forward one square.

Play the game and see which runner finishes first. Repeat the game a few times. Does the same runner always win? Is the game fair? Which runner is most likely to win? Which runner is least likely to win? Change the rules or board to make it fair.

Runners | | | | | | | | | | | Finishing line ↓
2											
3											
4											
5											
6											
7											
8											
9											
10											
11											
12											

Runners' lanes

TOPICS Triangles, quadrilaterals, congruence, vectors

Activity: Exploring shapes on geoboards

You will need:
- *nails*
- *pieces of wood*
- *string, cotton or elastic bands*

Make a few geoboards of different shapes and sizes. Students can wrap string or elastic around the nails to make different shapes on the geoboards like triangles, quadrilaterals. They can investigate the properties and areas of the different shapes.

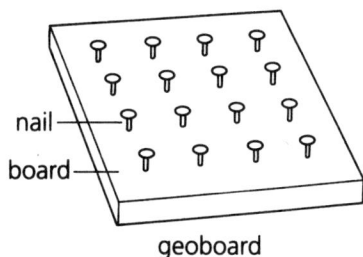

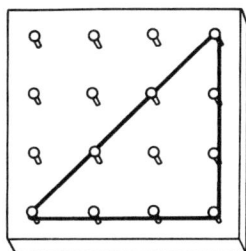

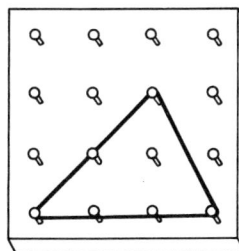

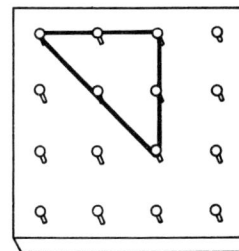

For example:
- How many different triangles can be found on a 3 × 3 geoboard? Classify the triangles according to: size of angles, length of sides, lines of symmetry, order of rotational symmetry. Find the area of the different triangles.

- How many different quadrilaterals can be made on 4 × 4 geoboards? Classify the quadrilaterals according to: size of angles, length of sides, lines of symmetry, order of rotational symmetry, diagonals. Find the area of the different quadrilaterals.

- How many different ways can a 4 × 4 geoboard be split into:
  - two congruent parts?
  - four congruent parts?

- Can you reach all the points on a 5 × 5 geoboard by using the three vectors shown? In how many different ways can these points be reached? Always start from the same point. You can use the three types of movement shown in the vectors in any order, and repeat them any number of times. Explore on different sized geoboards.

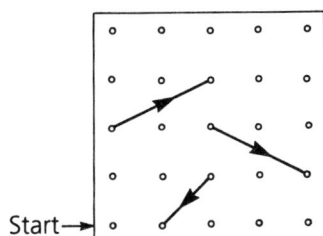

Problems and puzzles

This teaching method is about encouraging students to learn mathematics through solving problems and puzzles which have definite answers. The key point about problem-solving is that students have to work out the method for themselves.

Puzzles develop students' thinking skills. They can also be used to introduce some history of mathematics since there are many famous historical maths puzzles.

Textbook exercises usually get students to practise skills out of context. Problem-solving helps students to develop the skills to select the appropriate method and to apply it to a problem.

TOPIC Basic addition and subtraction

Activity: Magic squares

Put the numbers 1, 2, 3, 4, 5, 6, 7, 8, 9 into a 3 × 3 square to make a magic square. In this 3 × 3 magic square, the numbers in each

	8	

16	6	x
2	y	18
z	14	4

vertical row must add up to 15. The numbers in each horizontal row must add up to 15. The diagonals also add up to 15.15 is called the magic number.

- How many ways are there to put the numbers 1–9 in a magic 3 × 3 square?
- Can you find solutions with the number 8 in the position shown?
- There are 880 different solutions to the problem of making a 4 × 4 magic square using the numbers 1 to 16.
  How many of them can you find where the magic number is 34?
- What are the values of x, y and z in the magic square on the right? (The magic number is 30.)

TOPIC Multiplication and division of 3-digit numbers

1	9	2
3	8	4
5	7	6

Activity: Digits and squares

The numbers 1 to 9 have been arranged in a square so that the second row, 384, is twice the top row, 192. The third row, 576, is three times the first row, 192. Arrange the numbers 1 to 9 in another way without changing the relationship between the numbers in the three rows.

TOPIC The four operations on single-digit numbers

□	−	□	=	□
				×
□	÷	□	=	□
				=
□	+	□	=	□

Activity: Boxes

Put all the numbers 1 to 9 in the boxes so that all four equations are correct.

Fill in the boxes with a different set of numbers so that the four equations are still correct.

TOPIC Squaring numbers and adding numbers

► To square a number you multiply it by itself.

Activity: Circling the squares

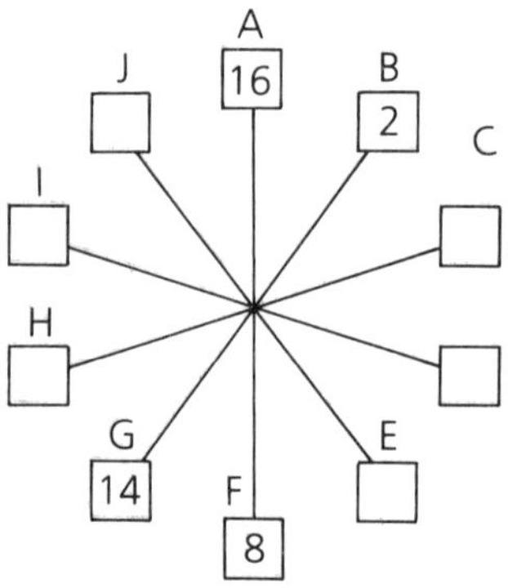

Place a different number in each empty box so that the sum of the squares of any two numbers next to each other equals the sum of the squares of the two opposite numbers.

For example: $16^2 + 2^2 = 8^2 + 14^2$

TOPIC Addition

Activity: Circling the sums

Put the numbers 1 to 19 in the boxes so that three numbers in a line add up to 30.

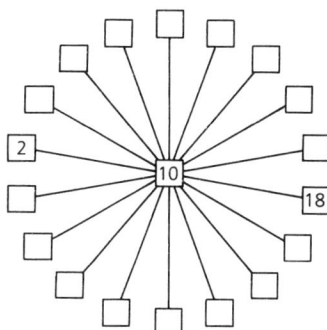

TOPIC *Surface area, volume and common factors*

Activity: The cuboid problem

The top of a box has an area of 120 cm², the side has an area of 96 cm² and the end has an area of 80 cm². What is the volume of the box?

TOPIC *Shape and symmetry*

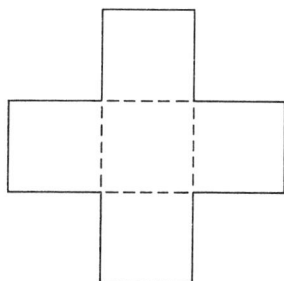

A Greek cross

Activity: The Greek cross

A Greek cross is made up of five squares, as shown in the diagram.

- Make a square by cutting the cross into five pieces and rearranging the pieces.
- Make a square by cutting the cross into four pieces and rearranging them.
- Try with pieces that are all the same size and shape. Try with all the pieces of different sizes and shapes.

TOPIC *Equilateral triangles and area*

▶ An equilateral triangle has three sides of equal length and three angles of equal size.

Activity: Match sticks

- Make four equilateral triangles using six match sticks.
- Take 18 match sticks and arrange them so that:
  - they enclose two spaces; one space must have twice the area of the other
  - they enclose two four-sided spaces; one space must have three times the area of the other
  - they enclose two five-sided spaces; one space must have three times the area of the other

TOPIC Addition, place value

$$
\begin{array}{r}
x\,x\,x \\
+y\,y\,y \\
+z\,z\,z \\
\hline
a\,b\,c\,d
\end{array}
\qquad
\begin{array}{r}
y \\
+y \\
+y \\
\hline
m\,y
\end{array}
$$

Activity: Decoding

Each letter stands for a digit between 0 and 9. Find the value of each letter in the sums shown.

TOPIC Forming and solving equations

Activity: Find the number

1 Find two whole numbers which multiply together to make 221.
2 Find two whole numbers which multiply together to make 41.
3 I am half as old as my mother was 20 years ago. She is now 38. How old am I?
4 Find two numbers whose sum is 20 and the sum of their squares is 208.
5 Find two numbers whose sum is 10 and the sum of their cubes is 370.
6 Find the number which gives the same result when it is added to $3\frac{3}{4}$ as when it is multiplied by $3\frac{3}{4}$.

TOPIC Percentages

Activity: Percentage problems

1 An amount increases by 20%. By what percentage do I have to decrease the new amount in order to get back to the original amount?
2 The length of a rectangle increases by 20% and the width decreases by 20%. What is the percentage change in the area?
3 The volume of cube A is 20% more than the volume of cube B. What is the ratio of the cube A's surface area to cube B's surface area?

TOPIC Probability

Activity: Probability problems

► To calculate the theoretical probability of an event, you need to list all the possible outcomes of the experiment.
► The theoretical probability of an event is the number of ways that event could happen divided by the number of possible outcomes of the experiment.

1 I have two dice. I throw them and I calculate the difference. What is the probability that the difference is 2? How about other differences between 0 and 6?
2 I write down on individual cards the date of the month on which everyone in the class was born. I shuffle the cards and choose two of them. What is the probability that the sum of the two numbers is even? What is the probability that the sum of the two numbers is odd? When would these two probabilities be the same?

3 Toss five coins once. If you have five heads or five tails you have won. If not, you may toss any number of coins two more times to get this result. What is the probability that you will get five heads or five tails within three tosses?

4 You have eight circular discs. On one side of them are the numbers 1, 2, 4, 8, 16, 32, 64 and 128. On the other side of each disc is a zero. Toss them and add together the numbers you see. What is the probability that the sum is at least 70?

5 Throw three dice. What is more likely: the sum of the numbers is divisible by 3 or the multiple of the numbers is divisible by 4?

Investigating mathematics

Many teachers show students how to do some mathematics and then ask them to practise it. Another very different approach is possible. Teachers can set students a challenge which leads them to discover and practise some new mathematics for themselves. The job for the teacher is to find the right challenges for students. The challenges need to be matched to the ability of the pupils.

The key point about investigations is that students are encouraged to make their own decisions about:
- where to start
- how to deal with the challenge
- what mathematics they need to use
- how they can communicate this mathematics
- how to describe what they have discovered.

We can say that investigations are open because they leave many choices open to the student. This section looks at some of the mathematical topics which can be investigated from a simple starting point. It also gives guidance on how to invent starting points for investigations.

TOPIC ## Linear equations and straight line graphs

- ▶ An equation can be represented by a graph.
- ▶ There is a relationship between the equation and the shape of the graph.
- ▶ A linear equation of the form $y = mx + c$ can be represented by a straight line graph.
- ▶ m determines the gradient of the straight line and c determines where the graph intercepts the y axis.

Investigation of graphs of linear equations

Write on the board:

The y number is the same as the x number plus 1.

Ask students to write down three pairs of co-ordinates which follow this rule. Plot the graph.

Change the rule:

The y number is the same as the x number plus 2.

Ask students to write down three pairs of co-ordinates which follow this rule. Plot the graph on the same set of axes.

Ask students what they notice about the gradients of the straight line graphs and the intercepts on the y axis.

Ask students to write the rules on the board as algebraic equations.

Students can then plot the graphs of the following rules:
- The y number = twice the x number
- The y number = three times the x number
- The y number = three times the x number plus 1

Ask students to write the rules as algebraic equations.

Students can work on their own to understand the relationship between straight line graphs and linear equations. The instructions below should help them.

Make your own rules for straight line graphs. Plot three co-ordinates and draw the graphs of these rules.

Make rules with negative numbers and fractions as well as whole numbers.

Write the equations for each rule and label each straight line graph with its equation.

Describe any patterns you notice about the gradient of the graphs and their intercept on the y axis. Do the equations of the graphs tell you anything about the gradient and the intercept on the y axis?

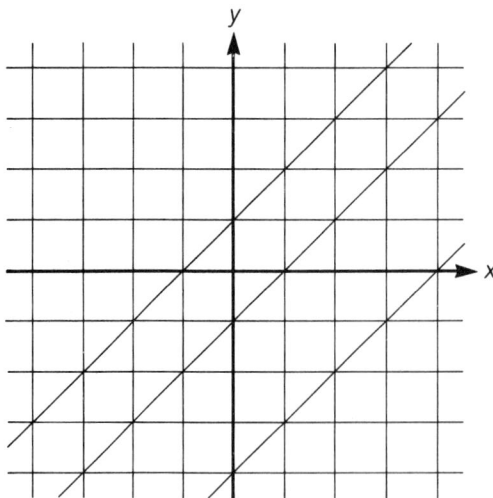

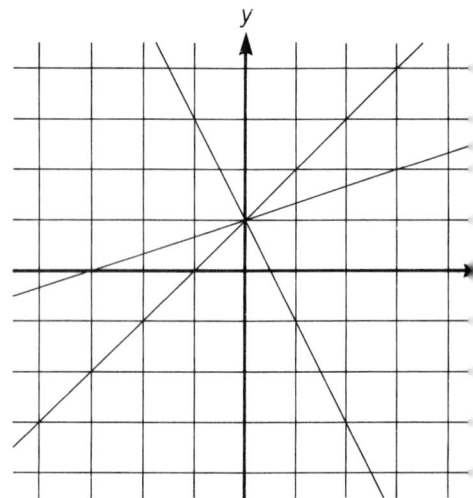

TOPIC Area and perimeter of shapes

- ▶ Area is the amount of space inside a shape.
- ▶ Perimeter is the distance around the outside of a shape.
- ▶ Area can be found by counting squares or by calculation for regular shapes.

Investigation of area and perimeter

1 A farmer has 12 logs to make a border around a field. Each log is 1 m long. The field must be rectangular.
What is the biggest area of field the farmer can make? What is the smallest area of field the farmer can make?
The farmer now has 14 logs. Each log is 1 m long. What are the biggest and smallest fields he can make?
Explore for different numbers of logs.

2 A farmer has 12 logs. Each log is 1 m long. A farmer can make a field of any shape.
What is the biggest area of field that the farmer can make? What is the smallest area of field the farmer can make?
Explore for different numbers of logs.

3 You have a piece of string that is 36 m long. Find the areas of all the shapes you can make which have a perimeter of 36 m.

4 A piece of land has an area of 100 m². How many metres of wire fencing is needed to enclose it?

TOPIC Volume and surface area of solids

► Volume is the amount of space a solid takes up.
► Volume can be found by counting cubes or by calculation for regular solids.
► Surface area is the area of the net of a solid.
► Surface area can be found by counting cubes or by calculation for regular shapes.

Investigation of volume and surface area of solids

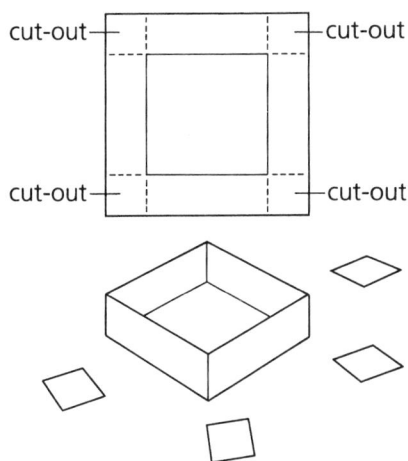

1 You may only use 1 sheet of paper. What is the largest volume cuboid you can make?

2 You are going to make a box which has a volume of 96 cm cubed or 96 cm³. The box can be any shape. What is the smallest amount of card you need?

3 You have a square of card. The card is 24 cm × 24 cm. You can make the card into a box by cutting squares out of the corners and folding the sides up.
Make the box with the biggest volume. What is the length of the side of the cut-out squares?
Try for other sizes of square card. Try with rectangular cards.

4 You have a piece of card which is 24 cm × 8 cm. The card is rectangular. What is the biggest volume cylinder you can make?

5 You are going to make a cylinder. The cylinder must have a volume of 80 cm³. What is the smallest amount of card you need?

TOPIC Simultaneous equations

► Simultaneous equations are usually pairs of equations with the same unknowns in both equations. For example:
$x + y = 10$
$x - y = 4$

► When simultaneous equations are solved, the unknowns have the same value for both equations. For example, in both equations above, $x = 7$ and $y = 3$.
One of the simultaneous equations cannot be solved without the other.

Investigation of simultaneous equations

Simultaneous equations can be solved by trial and improvement, by using equation laws and/or by substitution.

Write an equation on the top of the board, for example $x + y = 10$. Divide the rest of the board into two columns. Ask each student to do the following:
• Think of one set of values for x and y which makes the equation on the board true. Do not tell anyone these values.
• Make up another equation in x and y using your values.

Invite students one by one to say the equations they have made up. If their equation works with the same values as the teacher's equation, write it in the left hand column; if it does not work then write it in the right hand column. Ask students to:
• Work out the values of x and y for each set of equations.
• Discuss the methods they used to solve each set of simultaneous equations.

Study the two lists of equations on the board:
• Are any pairs the same?
• Can any of the equations be obtained from one or two others?

TOPIC *Tessellations*

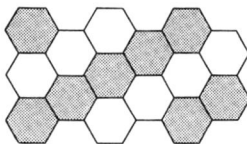

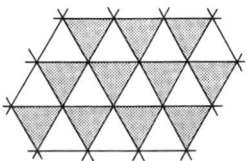

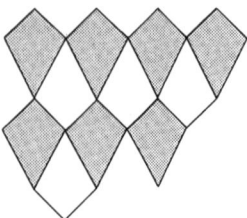

► A tessellation is a repeating pattern in more than one direction of one shape without any gaps.
► A semi-regular tessellation is a repeating pattern in more than one direction of two shapes without any gaps.
► A regular shape will tessellate if the interior angle is a factor of 360°.
► Semi-regular tessellations work if the sum of a combination of the interior angles of the two shapes is 360°.

Investigation of tessellations

Give students a collection of regular polygons. Ask them to find out:
• Which polygons can be used on their own to cover a surface without any gaps?
• Which two polygons can be used together to cover the surface without any gaps?
• Explain why some shapes tessellate on their own and others tessellate with a second shape.

TOPIC **The relationship between the circumference, radius, diameter and area of circles**

► The formula for the circumference of a circle is $2\pi r$
► The formula for the area of a circle is πr^2
► Assume that $\pi = 3.14$ for this exercise

Investigation of circles

You will need:
- *tins*
- *circular objects, for example plates, lids, pots*
- *cardboard circles of different sizes*

Measure the radius and the diameter of a variety of tins and circular objects. For each circle, work out a way to measure the area and circumference.

List all the results together in a table. Try to work out the relationship between:
- radius and diameter
- radius and circumference
- radius and area

radius	diameter	circumference	area

TOPIC **Fractions, decimals and percentages**

Investigation of fractions, decimals and percentages

Put 6 pieces of fruit on three tables as shown. Use the same kind of fruit, such as 6 apples or 6 bananas. Each piece of fruit must be roughly the same size.

Line up 10 students outside the room. Let them in one at a time. Each student must choose to sit at the table where they think they will get the most fruit.

Before the students enter, discuss the following questions with the rest of the class:
- Where do you think they will all want to sit?
- How much fruit will each student get?
- If students could move to another table, would they?
- Is it best to go first or last?
- Where is the best place to be in the queue?

When all 10 students are seated, ask students to do the following:
- Write down how much fruit each student gets. Write the amount as a fraction and as a decimal.
- Write down the largest amount of fruit any one student gets. Write this amount as a percentage of the total amount of fruit on the tables.

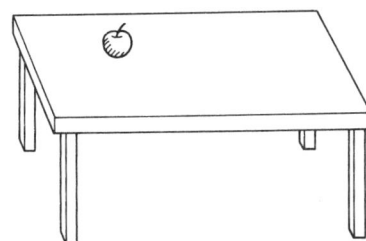

Repeat the activity with a different set of students sent outside the room. Try with a different number of tables or a different number of pieces of fruit or a different number of students.

TOPIC Line symmetry

▶ In a symmetrical shape every point has an image point on the opposite side of the mirror line at the same distance from it.

Investigation of symmetrical shapes

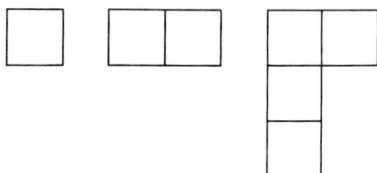

Make three pieces of card like the ones shown.

How many different ways can you put them together to make a symmetrical shape?

Draw in the line(s) of symmetry of each shape you make.

Now invent 3 simple shapes of your own and make up a similar puzzle for a friend to solve.

TOPIC Number patterns and arithmetic sequences

▶ A mathematical pattern has a starting place and one clear generating rule.
▶ Every number in a mathematical pattern can be described by the same algebraic term.

Investigation of number patterns

Fold a large piece of paper to get a grid. Label each box, as shown, according to its position in the row.

Choose a starting number and put it into the first box in Row 1.

Choose a generating rule, for example:
• Add 3 to the previous number.

Fill the row with the number pattern.

1	2	3	4	5	6
5	8	11	14	17	20

Choose other starting numbers and generating rules and create rows of number patterns.

1	2	3	4	5	6
10	20	30	40	50	60

Investigate the link between the label and number in the box.
For example:

Box	Number
1	10
2	20
3	30
etc.	

Which number would go in the 10th box of each number pattern in your grid? 100th box? nth box?

TOPIC Conducting statistical investigations: testing hypotheses, data collection, analysis and interpretation

Doing a statistical investigation

Hypothesis: Form 4 girls are fitter than Form 4 boys.

Step 1 Use a random sampling method to select 20 girls and 20 boys in Form 4.

Step 2 Decide how you will test fitness, for example:
- number of step-ups in one minute
- number of push-ups in one minute
- number of star jumps in one minute
- time taken to do 10 sit-ups
- pulse rate before any activity, immediately after activity, 1 minute after activity, 5 minutes after activity, 10 minutes after activity.

Step 3 Design a data collection sheet. Prepare a record sheet for the girls and a similar one for the boys.

Name of girl	Step-ups	Push-ups	Star jumps	Time for sit-ups
Marie	23	12	17	10
Anna	22	13	12	9
Susan				

Step 4 Collect necessary resources like a stop watch. Find a suitable time and place to conduct the fitness tests.

Step 5 Collect and record data. Make sure the tests are fair. For example, it may be unfair to test boys in the midday heat and girls in the late afternoon. To be fair, each girl and boy must go through the same tests, in the same order, under the same conditions.

Step 6 Analyse data by comparing the mean, mode, median and range of number of step-ups for girls and boys. Do the same for the number of push-ups, star jumps etc.
Is there a correlation between any of the activities? Could these be combined to give an overall fitness rating?

Step 7 Select ways of presenting the data in order to compare the fitness of girls and boys.

Step 8 Interpret the data. What are the differences between boys' and girls' performances on each test? Overall?

Step 9 Draw a conclusion.
Is it true that Form 4 girls are fitter than Form 4 boys? Is the hypothesis true or false?

Other hypotheses to test

Young people eat more sugar than old people.

The bigger the aeroplane, the longer it stays in the air.

Three times around your head is the same as your height.

The bigger the ball, the higher it bounces.

To test any hypothesis, each of the following steps must be carefully planned:

- Choose your sample.
  - How many people/aeroplanes/balls etc. will you include in your sample?
  - How will you select your sample so that your data is not biased?
- Choose a method of investigation:
  - Will you observe incidents in real life?
  - Will you need to do research, for example in the library to find out about the patterns of behaviour you are investigating?
  - Will you need to design a questionnaire or interview questions to get information from people like how much sugar they eat per day or per week?
  - Will you need to design an experiment such as drop five balls of different sizes from the same height and count the number of bounces?
- Decide how to record data in a user-friendly format.
- Make sure the data is collected accurately and without bias.
- Choose the measures to analyse and compare data.
  - Will you work with mean, median and/or mode?
  - Will range be helpful? Will standard deviation be useful?
- Choose how to present the relevant analysed data.
  - Will you use a table, bar chart, pie chart, line graph?
- Interpret the findings of your investigation.
- Draw a conclusion.
  - Is the hypothesis true or false? Is the hypothesis sometimes true?

CHAPTER 2 Resources and teaching aids

In this chapter we look at how you can use resources and practical activities to improve students' learning. We look at ways in which you can use a few basic resources such as bottle tops, sticks, matchboxes and string to teach important mathematical ideas and skills.

Why use resources and teaching aids

Spend some time thinking about the question:

What are the advantages and disadvantages of using resources, practical activities and teaching aids in the classroom?

Compare your ideas with the list below:

Advantages	**Disadvantages**
Actively involves students	Organising the activities
Motivates students	Monitoring work
Makes ideas concrete	Planning the work
Shows maths is in the real world	Assessment
Allows different approaches to a topic	Storing resources
Gives hands-on experience	Noisier classroom
Makes groupwork easier	Possible discipline problems
Gives opportunities for language development	

On balance, using resources and activities can greatly improve students' learning. The main difficulty from the teacher's point of view is organising, planning and monitoring the activities. We shall discuss these problems in Chapter 5.

What resources can be used?

Sticks, corks, bottle tops, cloth, matchboxes, envelopes, shells, string, rubber bands, drawing pins, beads, pebbles, shoe laces, buttons, old coins, seeds, pots and pans, washing line, newspaper, old magazines, paper and card, twigs, odd pieces of wood, old cardboard boxes and cartons, clay, tins, bags, bottles, people and most importantly, the mind!

There are many other things that you will be able to find around the school and local community.

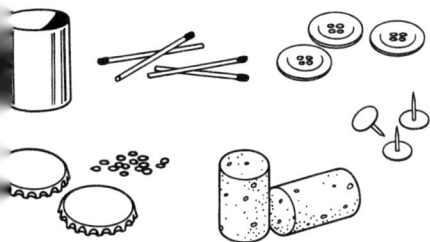

Making resources

Some resources take a long time to make but can be used again and again, others take very little time to make and can also be used again and again. But some resources can only be used once and you need to think carefully about whether you have the time to make them.

You also need to think about how many of each resource you need. Are there ways you can reduce the quantity? For example, can you change the organisation of your classroom so that only a small group of students use the resource at one time? Other groups can use the resource later during the week.

Get help with preparing and making resources. Here are some ideas:
• Students can make their own copies.
• Make resources with students in the maths club.
• Run a workshop with colleagues to produce resources. Share the resources with all maths teachers at the school.
• Invite members of the local community into the school to help make resources.
• Pace yourself. Make one set of resources a term. Build up a bank of resources over time.

Find ways of storing resources so that they are accessible and can be re-used. Perhaps one student can be responsible for making sure the resources are all there at the beginning and end of the lesson.

On the following pages, we give some mathematical starting points for using resources which don't need a great deal of work to prepare.

Using bottle tops

TOPIC *Reflection*

▶ Every point has an image point at the same distance on the opposite side of the mirror line.

Activity

You will need:
• *bottle tops*
• *small mirrors*
• *strips of card*

Place 5 bottle tops on a strip of card as shown.

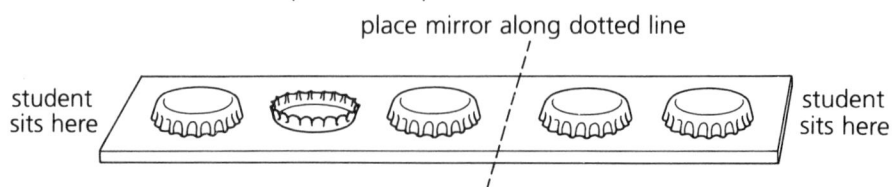
place mirror along dotted line

student sits here
student sits here

Place a mirror on the dotted line. One student sits at each end. Ask each other: What do you see? What do you think the other student sees? Move the mirror line. What do you see? What does the other student see?

Try different arrangements with double rows of bottle tops or different coloured bottle tops.

TOPIC Estimation

▶ Any unit of measurement can be compared with another unit of measurement, for example a metre can be compared with centimetres, inches, hands, bottletops etc.

Activity

Form two teams for a class quiz on estimation. Each team prepares a set of questions about estimation. For example:

How many bottle tops would fill a cup? a cooking pot? a wheelbarrow? a lorry?

How much would a lorry load of bottle tops weigh?

How many bottle tops side by side measure a metre? a kilometre? the length of the classroom?

Each team prepares the range of acceptable estimations for their set of questions. The team that makes the best estimations in the quiz wins.

TOPIC Co-ordinate pairs and transformations

▶ Co-ordinate pairs give the position of a point on a grid. The point with co-ordinate pair (2,3) has a horizontal distance of 2 and a vertical distance of 3 from the origin.
▶ Transformations are about moving and changing shapes using a rule. Four ways of transforming shapes are: reflection, rotation, enlargement and translation.

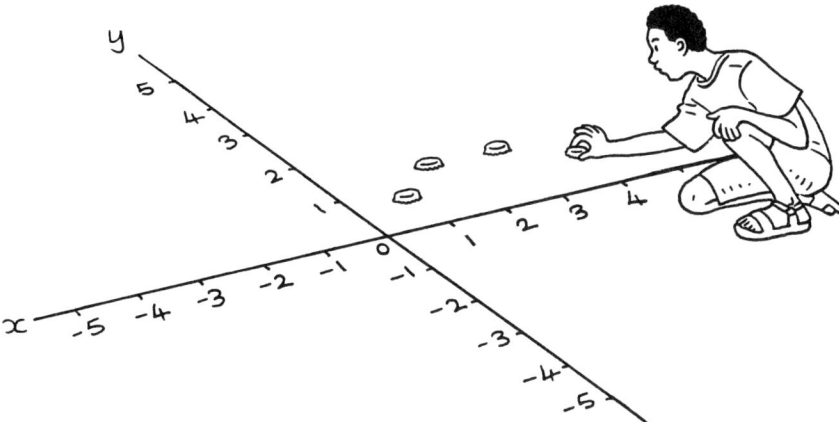

Activity for co-ordinates

Draw a large pair of axes on the ground or on a large piece of card on the ground. Label the y and x axes.

Place 4 bottle tops on the grid as the vertices (corners) of a quadrilateral. Record the 4 co-ordinate pairs. Make other quadrilaterals and record their co-ordinate pairs.

Sort the quadrilaterals into the following categories: square, rectangle, rhombus, parallelogram, kite, trapezium. In each category look for similarities between the sets of co-ordinate pairs.

Activities for transformations

▶ Reflection: every point has an image point at the same distance on the opposite side of the mirror line.

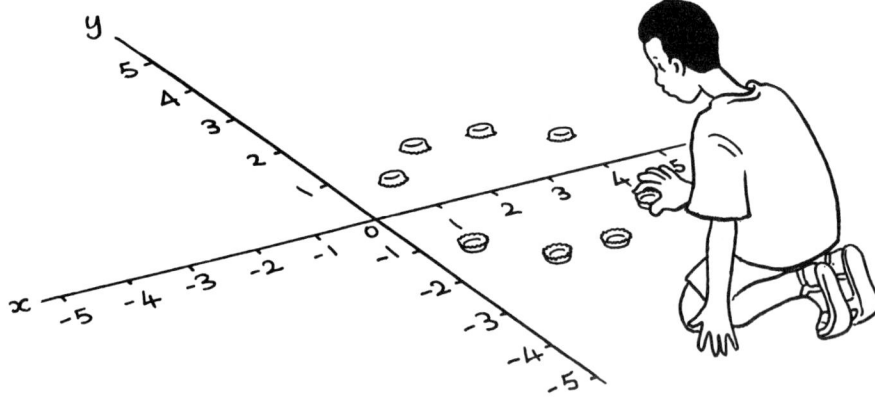

Place 4 bottle tops, top-side up, to make a quadrilateral. Record the co-ordinate pairs. Place another 4 bottle tops, teeth-side up, to show the mirror image of the first quadrilateral reflected in the line $y = 0$. Record these co-ordinate pairs. Compare the co-ordinate pairs of the first quadrilateral and the reflected quadrilateral.

Show different quadrilaterals reflected in the $y = 0$ line. Note the co-ordinates and investigate how the sets of co-ordinates are related.

Make reflections of quadrilaterals in other lines such as $x = 0$, $y = x$.

▶ Rotation: all points move the same angle around the centre of rotation.

Place bottle tops, top-side up, to make a shape. Record the co-ordinates of the corners of the shape. Place another set of bottle tops, teeth-side up, to show the image of the shape when it has been rotated 90° clockwise about the origin. Record these new co-ordinates. Compare the two sets of co-ordinate pairs.

Show different shapes rotated 90° clockwise about the origin. Note the co-ordinates and investigate how the sets of co-ordinates are related.

Now try rotations of other angles like 180° clockwise, 90° anti-clockwise.

▶ Enlargement: a shape is enlarged by a scale factor which tells you how many times larger each line of the new shape must be.

Place bottle tops, top-side up, to make a shape. Record the co-ordinates of the corners of the shape. Place another set of bottle tops, teeth-side up, to show the image of the shape when it has been enlarged by a scale factor of 2 from the origin. Record these new co-ordinates. Compare the two sets of co-ordinate pairs.

Show different shapes enlarged by a scale factor of 2 from the origin. Note the co-ordinates and investigate how the sets of co-ordinates are related.

Now try enlargements of other scale factors such as 5, $\frac{1}{2}$, −2. Try enlargements from points other than the origin.

▶ Translation: all points of a shape slide the same distance and direction.

Place bottle tops, top-side up, to make a shape. Record the co-ordinates of the corners of the shape. Place another set of bottle tops, teeth-side up, to show the image of the shape when it has been translated. Record these new co-ordinates. Compare the two sets of co-ordinate pairs.

Show different shapes translated. Note the co-ordinates and investigate how the sets of co-ordinates are related.

Now try different translations and see what happens.

TOPIC Combinations

▶ All possible outcomes can be listed and counted in a systematic way.

Activity

How many ways can you arrange three different bottle tops in a line?

Investigate for different numbers of bottle tops.

TOPIC Growth patterns, arithmetic progressions and geometric progressions

▶ A growth pattern is a sequence which increases by a given amount each time.
▶ Algebra can be used to describe the amount of increase.
▶ Arithmetic progressions have the same amount added each time.
▶ Geometric progressions have a uniformly increasing amount added each time.

Activity

Make Pattern 1 with bottle tops.

How many bottle tops in each pattern? How many bottle tops are added each time?

Complete the following, filling in the number of bottle tops per term:

Term 1: 1 *Term 2:* 1 + _ *Term 3:* 1 + _ + _ *Term 4:* 1 + _ + _ + _

Write the algebraic rule for the nth term.

Make each of the patterns on the next page with bottle tops. For each pattern, work out:
• the number of bottle tops in each term
• the amount of bottle tops added each time.

Work out the rule for the increase as an algebraic expression.

Write down the number of bottle tops in the 5th term, 8th term, nth term. Decide if each sequence is a geometric or arithmetic progression.

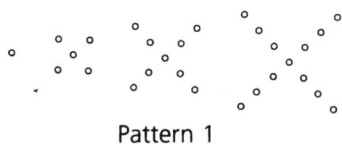

Pattern 1

Pattern 2	o	oo	ooo	oooo

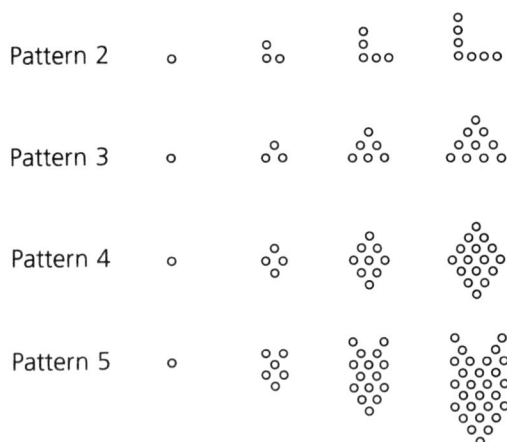

Make up some growth patterns of your own to investigate.

TOPIC Loci

▶ A locus is the set of all possible positions of a point, given a rule.
▶ The rule may be that all points must be the same distance from a fixed point, a line, 2 lines, a line and a point etc.

Activity

You will need:
- *a collection of bottle tops*
- *chalk*

- Put one bottle top top-side up on the floor. Place the other bottle tops teeth-side up so that they are all the same distance from the one that is top-side up.
- Draw a line on the floor. Place the bottle tops so that they are all the same distance from the line.
- Put two bottle tops, top-side up, on the floor. Place the other bottle tops, teeth-side up, so that they are all the same distance from both the tops which are top-side up.
- Draw two intersecting straight lines on the floor. Place several bottle tops so that they are all the same distance from both lines.
- What does the locus of points look like for each of the above rules?

Using sticks

TOPIC Growth patterns

▶ A growth pattern is a sequence which increases by a given amount each time.
▶ Algebra can be used to describe the amount of increase.
▶ A formula in algebra can be used to describe all terms in a pattern.

Activity

Use matchsticks or twigs to create this triangle pattern.

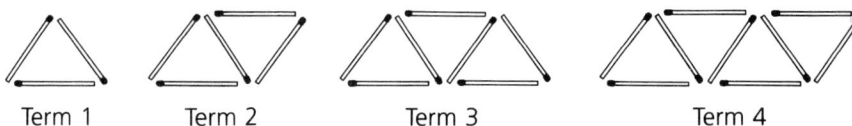

Term 1   Term 2   Term 3   Term 4

Figure 2.6

How many triangles and how many sticks in each term of the pattern?

How many sticks are added in each term?

How many triangles will there be in the 5th term? 8th term? 60th term? nth term?

How many sticks will there be in the 5th term? 8th term? nth term?

Investigate the relationship between the number of sticks and the number of triangles.

Explore the relationship between the number of sticks and the number of squares in the two patterns below.

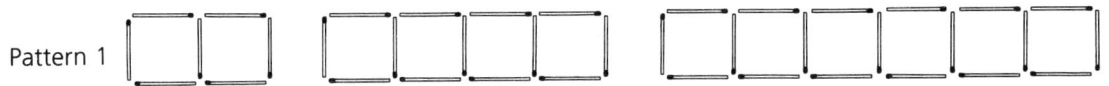

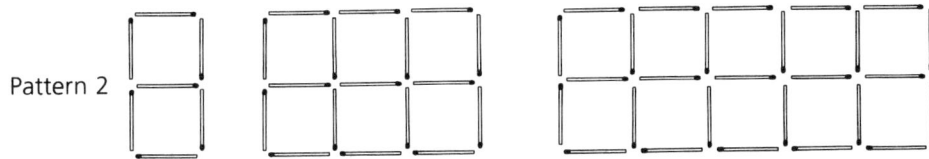

Pattern 1

Pattern 2

- Quadratic patterns
  How many sticks in a 1×1 square? a 2×2 square? a 3×3 square? an $n \times n$ square?

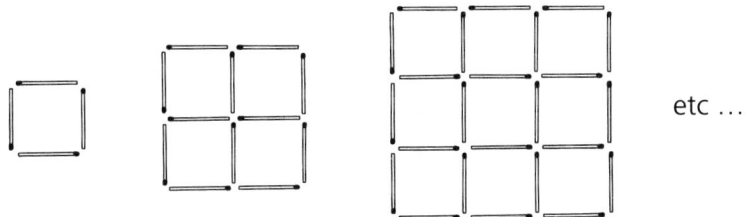

  etc …

- How many sticks for an $n \times n \times n$ triangle?

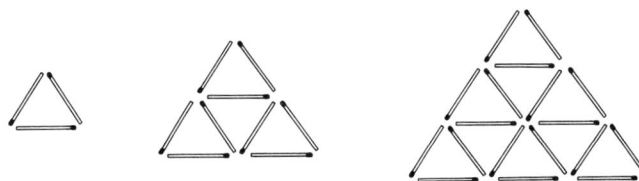

- Is there a number of sticks that will form both a square and a triangle pattern?

TOPIC Area and perimeter

► Area is the amount of space inside a flat shape.
► Perimeter is the distance around the outside of a flat shape.

Activity

• Use the same number of sticks for the perimeter of each rectangle. Create two rectangles so that:
  – the area of one is twice the area of the other
  – the area of one is four times the area of the other.
• Use the same number of sticks to form two quadrilaterals so that the area of one is three times the area of the other.

TOPIC Standard and non-standard units of measurement

► We can measure length, area, volume, mass, capacity, temperature and time.
► Non-standard units of measurement differ from place to place.
► Standard units of measurement are used in many places.
► Most countries use the metric system of units.

Common standard units of measurement:

Length	metres, millimetres, kilometres
Area	square kilometres, hectares
Volume	cubic metres, cubic centimetres
Mass	grams, kilograms, tonnes
Capacity	litres, millilitres
Temperature	degrees Celsius
Time	seconds, minutes, hours, days

Activities to explore non-standard units

• In groups of four, think of four different non-standard units to measure length, for example an exercise book, a local non-standard unit, a handspan. Estimate and then measure the length of various things with all four non-standard units. For example, measure the dimensions of the doors and windows in the classroom, the height of your friends etc.

• Use four sticks of different lengths. Measure various things with the different sticks.
  Which stick is best for which object? Why?

• Find four different non-standard containers like tins, bottles, cups. Measure different amounts of liquid (such as water) and solids (such as sand, grain) with the different measures.

• What non-standard units would be useful to measure mass?

• What units are used in local markets and shops?

Activities to explore standard units

- Make sticks of different lengths of standard units such as 1 cm, 5 cm, 100 cm and 1 metre. Use them to estimate and measure the lengths of various things. Which stick is best for which object?

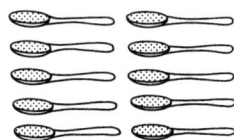

Activities to compare standard and non-standard measures

- Compare the measurements made using non-standard units with those measurements made using standard units. For example:
  How many cups are equal to one litre?
  How many handspans are equal to one metre?
- Are any non-standard units particularly useful? Draw up a table which shows the relationship between a useful non-standard unit and a standard unit.

10 spoons fill 1 cup

$3\frac{1}{2}$ bottles fill 1 bucket

Using Cuisenaire rods

TOPIC Algebraic manipulation

- ▶ equivalences: $2(3a + b) = 6a + 2b = 3a + b + 3a + b = \dots$, etc
- ▶ basic conventions: $a + a + a = 3a$, and $3b - 2b + 5b = 6b$
- ▶ collecting like terms and simplifying:
  $2a + 3b + 4a + c = 6a + 3b + c$
- ▶ The add-subtract law: $a + b = c$, $a = c - b$, $b = c - a$ are all equivalent
- ▶ the subtracting bracket laws: $a - (b \pm c) = a - b \mp c$
- ▶ commutativity: $a + b = b + a$ but $a - b \neq b - a$
- ▶ associativity: $a + (b + c) = (a + b) + c$, $a - (b - c) \neq (a - b) - c$
- ▶ multiplying out brackets: $3(2a + b) = 6a + 3b$
- ▶ factorising: $4a + 2b = 2(2a + b)$

Cuisenaire rods take a long time to make but can be used for many activities, last for years and can be shared by everyone in the maths department.

Choose a lot of sticks that are about the same diameter; bamboo is ideal. Cut them into lengths and colour them so that you have:

50 w	rods	1 cm long coloured white
50 r	rods	2 cm long coloured red
40 g	rods	3 cm long coloured light green
40 p	rods	4 cm long coloured pink
40 y	rods	5 cm long coloured yellow
40 d	rods	6 cm long coloured dark green
30 b	rods	7 cm long coloured black
30 t	rods	8 cm long coloured brown
30 B	rods	9 cm long coloured blue
20 O	rods	10 cm long coloured orange

Activity 1

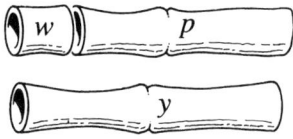

Two or more rods laid end to end make a rod train. The rod train made from a pink rod and a white rod is the same length as the yellow rod.

Find all the different rod trains equal in length to a yellow rod. List your answers. Then make trains equal in length to other colour rods.

Activity 2

In this activity:

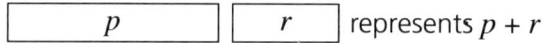 represents $p + r$

 represents $p - r$

Answer the following questions using your set of Cuisenaire rods. For these questions your answer should always be a single rod.

Question 8

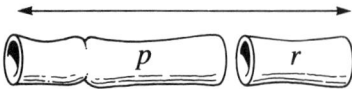

Question 21

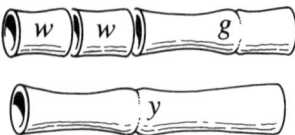

1   $t - p = \square$

2   $g + r + y = \square$

3   $\square + r = y$

4   $y - \square = g$

5   $t = r + \square$

6   $O - t = \square$

7   $y + g - d = \square$

8   $\square = r + p$

9   $t - y = \square$

10   $g + r = \square$

11   $y - r = \square$

12   $y - (r + r) = \square$

13   $(y + r) - g = \square$

14   $y - (r + \square) = r$

15   $y - g - \square = w$

16   $w + r + \square = p$

17   $t - (\square + w) = g$

18   $\square - (b + r) = w$

19   $p - g = \square$

20   $w + g + g + \square = B$

21   $2w + g = \square$

22   $w + 3g = \square$

23   $4w + 2g = \square$

24   $y + r = 2r + w + \square$

25   $d = \square + w$

26   $\square = g + d$

27   $B - (2r + p) = \square$

28   $y = 3w + \square$

29   $w + \square + y = b$

30   $O - 2r = \square$

31   $d + (b - 2g) = \square$

32   $w + r + \square + w = y$

33   $g + p = \square$

34   $B - b + r = \square$

35   $\square = O - (2r + g)$

36   $b - \square = r$

37   $b - (w + \square + g) = r$

38   $3y - 2p = \square$

39   $B - 2\square = g$

40   $y - 4\square = w$

41   $O - 3\square = p$

42   $3y - 2(r + w) = \square$

43   $3y - 2r - 2w = \square$

44   $3y - 2r = \square + 2w$

45   $3y = \square + 2w + 2r$

46   $\frac{1}{2}$ of $(3y - \square) = r + w$

Activity 3

Test the following to see if they are true or false.

1 $r + g = g + r$
2 $w + r + g = r + w + g$
3 $3r = r + 2r$
4 $y - r = r - y$
5 $r + (p + y) = (r + p) + y$

6 $b - (r + w) = b - r - w$
7 $b - 2r = b - r - r$
8 $(b + y) - p = b + (y - p)$
9 $(t - p) - w = t - (p - w)$
10 $3y - 2p = (2y - p) + (y - p)$

Now make up some of your own to test.

Activity 4

Lay out the *red* and *green* Cuisenaire rods end to end as a rod train:

r	g

Do this again so you have all 4 rods lying end to end as one rod train:

r	g	r	g

This is 2 lots of (red + green) or 2 $(r + g)$

You can lay the rods out in many ways. For instance:

$r + r + g + g$ or $2r + 2g$

$g + 2r + g$

Since these rod trains all use the same rods, you can say that they are **equivalent**.

So you can write:

$$\begin{aligned} 2(r + g) &= r + r + g + g \\ &= 2r + 2g \\ &= g + 2r + g \end{aligned}$$

- Write down as many other equivalent forms to $2(r + g)$ as you can.
- Set up each of the following with rods. For each case, set up and write down as many equivalent forms as you can.

1 $2(g + p)$
2 $3(g + y)$
3 $3(2w + g)$

4 $2(3r + 2p)$
5 $3(g + 2p + 3r)$

Activity 5

You can do something similar when you have subtraction signs.
The yellow minus the red is set up as follows:

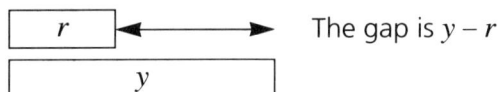

The gap is $y - r$

Doing this twice you get:

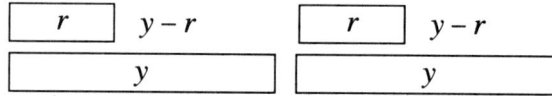

| r | $y - r$ |

| r | $y - r$ |

| y |

| y |

The total gap is $(y - r) + (y - r)$ or $2(y - r)$

If you move a *red* rod across you can have:

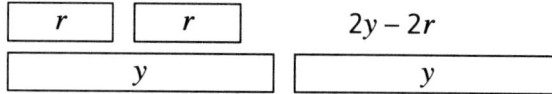

| r | r |

$2y - 2r$

| y |

| y |

or that gap could be:

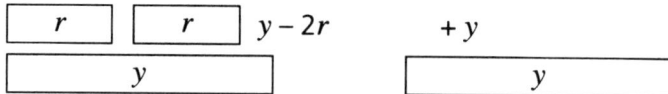

| r | r | $y - 2r$

$+ y$

| y |

| y |

So, since all the gaps are of the same length, you can say that
$(y - r) + (y - r)$
$2(y - r)$
$2y - 2r$
$y - 2r + y$
are all equivalent forms.

- Can you find any more equivalent forms to $2(y - r)$?
  Write them all down if you can.
- Set up each of the following with rods. Write down as many
  equivalent forms as you can for each one.

  1 $2(b - p)$ **4** $3(2y - g)$
  2 $3(y - r)$ **5** $3(4y - 3g)$
  3 $2(2g - r)$

Activity 6

You have seen that $2(r + g) = 2r + 2g$

When you go from $2(r + g)$ to $2r + 2g$ it is called **multiplying out**.

When you go from $2r + 2g$ to $2(r + g)$ it is called **factorising**.

These are special equivalent forms. You can use rods for the next set
of questions, or do without them.

- Multiply out:

  1 $3(y + b)$ **6** $5(3p - y)$
  2 $2(3p + w)$ **7** $4(3b + 2g)$
  3 $4(2y + B)$ **8** $3(2y + r - g)$
  4 $3(g + w)$ **9** $5(3t - 2b)$
  5 $3(4w - g)$ **10** $4(3p + 2w - 3g)$

- Factorise

1	$2g + 2w$	**6**	$4y + 6p$
2	$3g - 3r$	**7**	$5y - 5w$
3	$3b - 6w$	**8**	$6g + 9w$
4	$4g + 2w$	**9**	$2p + 4g + 6r$
5	$3t + 9r$	**10**	$3y - 6g + 3p$

- Do these without rods. Write down as many equivalent forms as you can.

1	$2(x + y)$	**6**	$x + 2y + 3x + 5y$
2	$3(x + y)$	**7**	$2x + 3y - x - y$
3	$2(3x + y)$	**8**	$3y + 7x - y - 3x$
4	$3(2x - y)$	**9**	$x + y + 4x - 2y + 2y + 3y$
5	$5(2x + 3y)$	**10**	$3x - y + 2x + 6y$

Activity 7

Solve the equations.

1	$g + r + y = \square$	**14**	$b - (w + \square + g) = r$
2	$y + g - d = \square$	**15**	$2\square = d$
3	$t - \square + w = b$	**16**	$2\square + g = b$
4	$(y + r) - g = \square$	**17**	$2\square - p = d$
5	$y - (r + \square) = r$	**18**	$3\square - t = O$
6	$\square - (b + r) = w$	**19**	$5\square + p = B$
7	$w + g + g + \square = B$	**20**	$4\square - B = b$
8	$y + r = 2r + w + \square$	**21**	$3\square + y = O + b$
9	$B - (2r + p) = \square$	**22**	$4\square + p = O + d$
10	$w + \square + y = b$	**23**	$\square + r = 2\square - r$
11	$d + (b - 2g) = \square$	**24**	$\square + g = 2\square - r$
12	$2w + r + \square = y$	**25**	$3\square - r = \square + p$
13	$\square = O - (2r + g)$	**26**	$3\square = \square + t$

Activity 8

Test the following to see if they are true or false.

1	$r + g = g + r$	**6**	$O - (y + p) = O - y - p$
2	$(w + p) + g = w + (p + g)$	**7**	$B - (r + w) = B - r - w)$
3	$2(g + w) = 2g + w$	**8**	$(w + O) - y = w + (O - y)$
4	$y - r = r - y$	**9**	$B - 2r = B - r + r$
5	$r + (y - p) = (r + y) - p$	**10**	$(b + y) - p = b + (y - p)$

Now try to write $6p - 4y$ in at least 5 different ways.

Using matchboxes

TOPIC ## Surface area and nets of rectangular solids

▶ The surface area of a solid is the sum of the areas of all the faces of the solid.

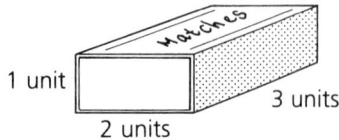

Activity

Calculate the surface area of a closed matchbox.

1 unit

2 units

3 units

How many squares 1 unit $\square$ 1 unit would cover the matchbox?

How many different nets of the matchbox are there?

Put two matchboxes together. How many different cuboids can you make? What is the smallest surface area?

Investigate the smallest surface area of a cuboid made from:
• three matchboxes
• four matchboxes
• eight matchboxes

TOPIC ## Length and area scale factors

▶ When you increase the lengths of the sides of a shape by a scale factor, the area of the shape is increased by the square of the scale factor.

Activity

Construct a giant matchbox which is three times the size of an ordinary matchbox.

What is the area of each side of the giant matchbox?

Explore the lengths and areas of other sized matchboxes.

Pythagoras' Theorem
$a^2 = b^2 + c^2$

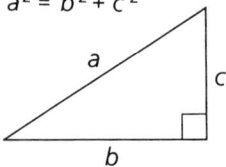

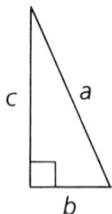

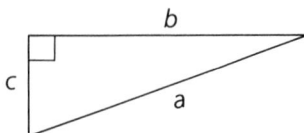

TOPIC ## Area of rectangles and Pythagoras' Theorem

▶ The area of a rectangle is equal to length × width.
▶ Pythagoras' theorem states $a^2 = b^2 + c^2$ when a is the side opposite the right angle in a right-angled triangle

Activity

$a^2 = b^2 + c^2$

• In each picture at the top of page 45, a rectangular piece of stiff card is placed inside the tray of a matchbox.

Measure the sides of a matchbox tray. Use these dimensions and Pythagoras' Theorem to work out the dimensions of the rectangular pieces of card in each picture.

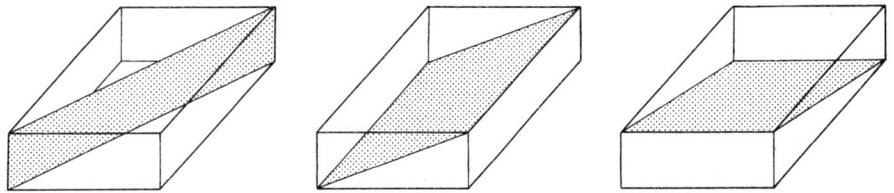

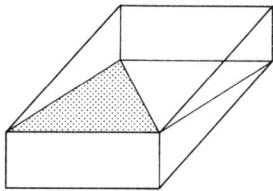

When you have worked out the length and width of each rectangle, cut the rectangles to size and see if they fit into a matchbox tray. Did you calculate the sides of the rectangles correctly?

Calculate the area of each rectangle. Which has the largest area?

- What is the largest triangle that can fit inside a matchbox?
- What is the formula for the area of a triangle?

TOPIC **Views and perspectives**

- ▶ 3-D, or three-dimensional, solids can be looked at from above, the side or the front.
- ▶ These views can be drawn in two dimensions as plans and elevations.
- ▶ 3-D solids can also be drawn using isometric drawing.

Activity

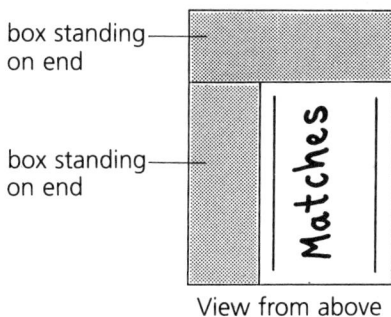

- Here is a top view of a solid shape made from three matchboxes. Make the structure from three matchboxes. Draw the side and front views.

- Make your own matchbox structure using 4 matchboxes. For each structure, draw the top view. Give the top view to another student. Ask him/her to make the structure and draw the side and front views.
- Make a matchbox structure from three matchboxes so that the top, side and front views are all the same.
- How many different top views can be made using three matchboxes? Explore for different numbers of matchboxes.

box standing on end

box standing on end

Matches

View from above

TOPIC **Combinations**

- ▶ All possible outcomes can be listed and counted in a systematic way.

Activity

Here are some different ways of arranging three matchboxes.

How many different ways can you find?

Record and count all the different arrangements in a systematic way.

Work with other numbers of matchboxes, for example five. List and count all the possible different arrangements of the matchboxes. Find ways of recording your work.

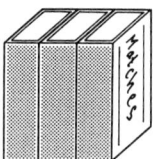

Using string

TOPIC Ordering whole numbers, fractions and decimals

▶ Place value uses the position (place) of a digit to give it its value.
For example:
In 329, the 3 has the value of 300 as it is in the hundreds column.
In 0.034, the 3 has a value of three hundredths as it is in the hundredths column.

Activity

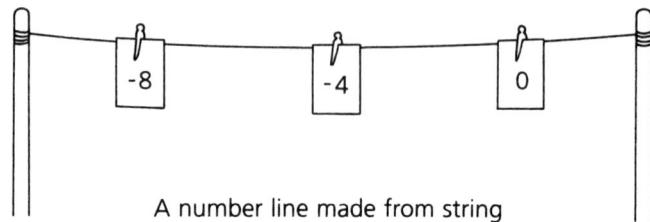

A number line made from string

• Tie a piece of string to make a straight line across the classroom.
This represents the number line. Use clothes pegs to peg the following numbers in the correct place on the line.

$\boxed{10}$ $\boxed{11}$ $\boxed{23}$ $\boxed{15}$ $\boxed{4}$ $\boxed{0}$ $\boxed{25}$ $\boxed{1}$

• Make five more cards, some with negative numbers. Peg the cards in the correct place on the number line.

• Peg the cards $\boxed{0}$ and $\boxed{1}$ at either end of the number line. Make cards which fit on this number line. Peg them in the correct places. Where will you peg the cards you made if the ends are labelled 0 and 100? 4 and 4.5? 0.1 and 0.2? 10 000 and 1 000 000? $\frac{1}{2}$ and $\frac{3}{4}$?

• Put $\boxed{19}$ in the middle. What could be at each end of the number line?
What if $\boxed{0.7}$ is in the middle? $\boxed{\frac{3}{8}}$? $\boxed{-23}$?
What could be at the ends of the number line in each case?

• Make sets of cards to show the two times table: 2, 4, 6, 8 up to 24. Put them on the number line with the correct spacing. Predict what the spacing will be for other times tables. Try them out. What about the spacing of sets of numbers 1, 2, 4, 8, 16, …

TOPIC Probability

▶ Probability is about the likelihood of an event happening.
▶ To describe the likelihood of an event happening, we use probability words like:
very likely, evens, certain, unlikely, impossible, probable.

Activity

• Tie a piece of string to make a straight line across the classroom. Peg cards $\boxed{0}$ and $\boxed{1}$ on the ends of the line. This is a

| It will rain tomorrow. | I will go to school tomorrow. | I will throw a 6 on a die. |

probability line that goes from 0 (impossible) to 1 (certain). Using clothes pegs, peg cards on the line to show the likelihood of different future events. Make up events of your own and put them on cards on the line.

- Discuss where these cards should be placed on the probability line.

| evens | very likely | good chance | dead certain | possible | unlikely | definite | no chance |

TOPIC Ratio

- ▶ Ratio is the comparison of two quantities or measurements.
- ▶ Ratios are written as follows:
  $a{:}b$; age:height; 2:3
- ▶ Ratio shows how many times bigger or smaller one thing is compared with another.

Activity: Body parts

Make a list of body parts that can be measured with a piece of string like
- circumference of the wrist
- circumference of the neck
- circumference of the base of the thumb
- circumference of the waist
- distance from shoulder to finger tip
- height
- circumference of head

Cut a length of string the same length as each body part in the list.

Find the ratio of:
- thumb:wrist
- wrist:neck

Investigate other body ratios. Record your findings by calling the thumb 1.

What about other body ratios:
- nose length:thumb length?
- half a head:height?

Measuring half a head

TOPIC Fractions

- ▶ Different fractions can describe the same number: e.g. $\frac{1}{2} = \frac{50}{100} = \frac{36}{72}$. These are called equivalent fractions.

▶ When a whole has been split into equal pieces, some of the pieces can be taken away. We can describe this using fractions.

Activity

- Take a piece of string, fold it in half. Mark or cut the fold. Fold it in half again and again and again.
  Look for equivalent fractions. Write some equivalence sentences like $\frac{4}{8} = \frac{2}{4}$.
- Fold a piece of string into 8 equal pieces. Cut off $\frac{1}{8}$. Write some subtraction sentences with $\frac{1}{8}$ such as
  $$1 - \frac{1}{8} = \frac{7}{8}$$
  $$\frac{1}{2} - \frac{1}{8} = \frac{3}{8}$$
- Repeat with another piece of string for the $\frac{1}{3}$, $\frac{1}{6}$, $\frac{1}{12}$ family.

TOPIC *Straight line graphs*

▶ Straight line graphs represent linear functions.
▶ The general equation of a straight line graph is $y = mx + c$.
  m is the gradient of the straight line graph.
  c is where the graph crosses the y axis.
▶ Straight line graphs that are parallel have the same gradient. Straight line graphs that cross the y axis at the same point have the same value for c.

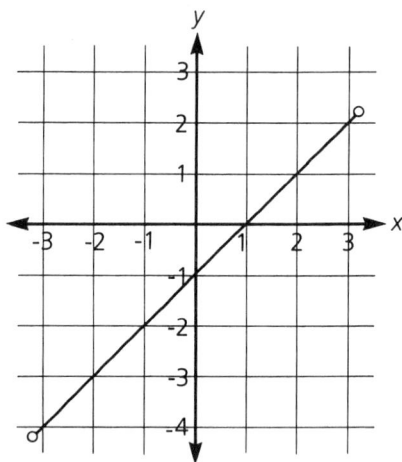

Activity

Make a large grid on a big piece of card, paper or chalkboard. Draw a pair of axes. Use a piece of string to represent a straight line graph. Invite students to pin pieces of string on to the grid to represent different sets of linear functions.

- Pin pieces of string on the grid to represent the following sets of equations:

$y = x$	$y = x + 1$	$y = 1$	$x = 2$
$y = x + 1$	$y = 2x + 1$	$y = 0$	$x = 0$
$y = x + 4$	$y = 4x + 1$	$y = 4$	$x = -3$
$y = x - 2$	$y = \frac{x}{2} + 1$	$y = -2$	$x = \frac{1}{2}$
	$y = -2x + 1$		

- Use two pieces of string to represent and solve simultaneous linear equations like
  $$y = 2x + 6$$
  $$y = 2$$

Constructions with string

▶ Constructions are about drawing lines, angles and shapes without measuring angles or lengths.

Activity

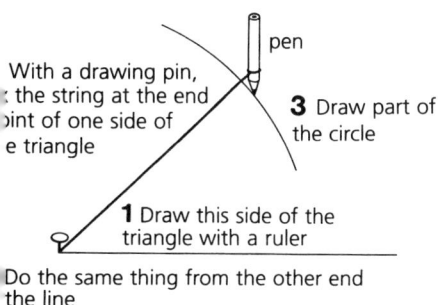

With a drawing pin, the string at the end point of one side of e triangle

pen

3 Draw part of the circle

1 Draw this side of the triangle with a ruler

Do the same thing from the other end the line

- Use a piece of string instead of a pair of compasses to construct:
  - an equilateral triangle
  - an isosceles triangle

- Use string to construct an ellipse. Explore what happens when you change the distance between the drawing pins and the length of the string.

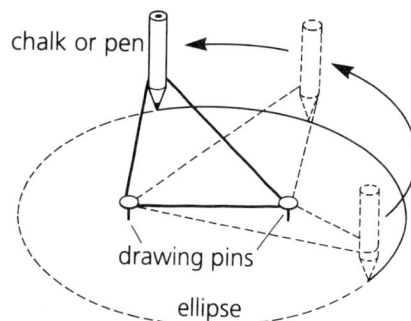

chalk or pen

drawing pins

ellipse

Mappings and functions

▶ A mapping is a rule connecting a set of elements in one set to other elements in another set.
▶ A function is a special sort of mapping. It is a one-to-one mapping. For each element in one set there is a unique element in the other set.
▶ Mappings and functions can be shown in diagrams and graphs. The rule of a mapping or a function can be described using algebra.

You will need:
- *thick card or cardboard or part of an old box*
- *a sharp point such as a nail or a knitting needle*

Activity

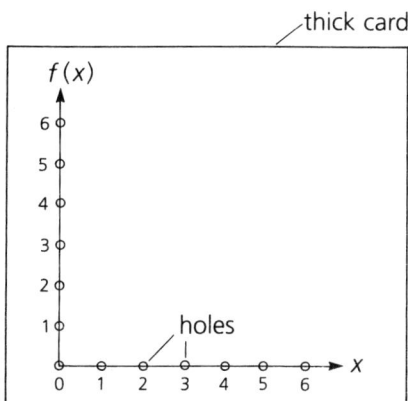

thick card

$f(x)$

holes

On the card draw axes, label them, put on the scales and carefully make a hole at each point.

- Represent the function $f(x): x \rightarrow 7 - x$ on this board.
  Write down the co-ordinates of points that are mapped together.
  For example $1 \rightarrow 7 - 1$ gives $(1,6)$.
  Join up the points by threading string through the holes.

- Try to show the mappings of the following rules:
  $f(x): x \rightarrow 6 - x$
  $f(x): x \rightarrow 3 - x$
  Explore for $f(x): x \rightarrow k - x$. Try with values of x.

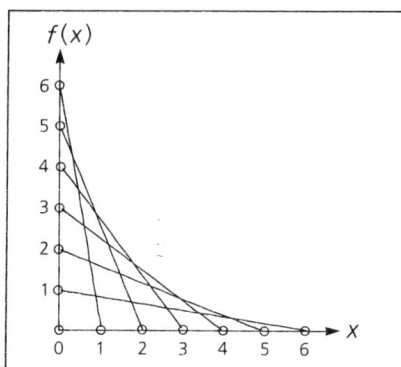

$f(x)$

- Fasten two long sticks or pieces of wood so that they are about half a metre apart. Put a number line on each stick and hammer in a nail on each number. Label one stick x and the other stick $f(x)$.

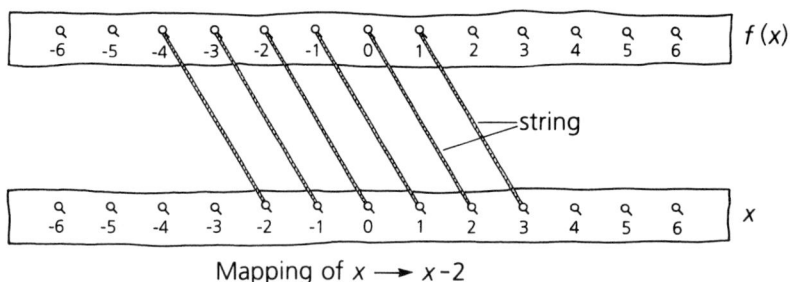

Mapping of $x \longrightarrow x-2$

Show mappings by joining up the numbers using string, as in the example above.

Show the following mappings:
$$f(x){:}x \rightarrow x - 3$$
$$f(x){:}x \rightarrow x + 4$$
$$f(x){:}x \rightarrow 2x$$
Make up and show your own mappings.

Using your imagination – mental imagery

TOPIC Loci

▶ Locus of a point is equidistant from two fixed points.
▶ Types of triangles: right-angled, obtuse, equilateral.

Mental imagery is particularly useful for teaching loci because it conveys the idea of movement.

Activity: Three points

- Imagine three points. Put them on a straight line. Move the middle point back and forth between the other two points. Then place it half way between them.
- Now move the middle point off the straight line joining the other two, but keep it always the same distance from each of them. Keep moving the point, but always equidistant from the other two points. Describe what sort of path it takes.
- Imagine straight lines joining the three points. What sort of triangle are you making as the middle point moves?
- Now let the middle point continue moving. What sort of triangle are you making?Can you make the triangle equilateral? What happens to the triangle when the third point comes back to the line between the other two?

TOPIC Trigonometry

▶ Trigonometry uses the ratios between the lengths of the sides of a right-angled triangle for a given angle.
▶ These ratios are called sine, cosine and tangent. They can be found listed in a book of tables.
▶ The ratios can be used to solve problems involving right-angled triangles.

Activity: Sine

You will need:
• *chalkboard*
• *ruler*
• *book of tables*

Draw the diagram on the chalkboard.

Give students the following instructions:
• Imagine the red radius is moving anticlockwise. Move it right round the circle.

• Now move it again, but watch the dotted line. Look how the length of the line changes as the angle increases from 0° to 90°.
• Now move the radius from 90° to 180°. What happens to the length of the dotted line?
• Complete the circle, watching how the length of the dotted line changes.
• Put the red radius at 30° and notice the length of the dotted line. What other angles give the same length?
• At what angles does the dotted line have no length?
• At what angles does the dotted line have the same length as the radius?
• Sketch a graph of how the length of the dotted line changes as the radius moves from 0° to 360°.
• When the length of the red radius is 1, the length of the dotted line is called the sine of the angle. Use the book of tables to plot the graph accurately.
• Look at the chalkboard again. If the length of the radius is 3 times as long, what happens to the length of the dotted line? If the radius is 10 times as long, what happens to the length of the dotted line?

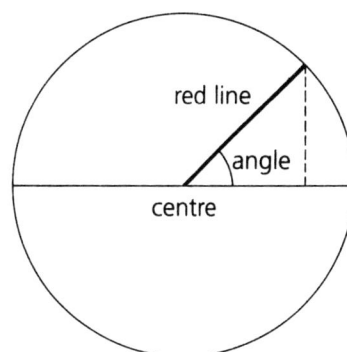

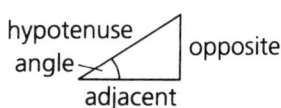

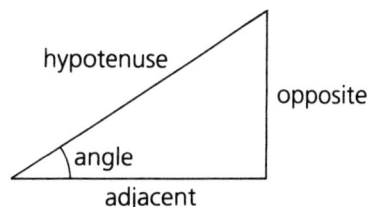

▶ The hypotenuse represents the scale factor. So:

Length of the hypotenuse × sine of the angle = length of the opposite side.

Activity: Cosine

Add the blue line to the chalkboard diagram.

Repeat the activity above, but imagine how the length of the blue line changes as the red radius moves round the circle.

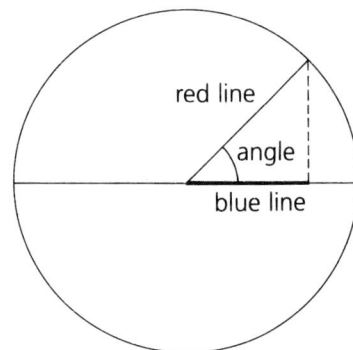

▶ This will lead to the idea that:

Length of the hypotenuse × cosine of the angle = length of the adjacent side.

TOPIC Geometry of a cube

▶ A cube has 6 faces, 8 vertices and 12 edges. Solid shapes can be classified by the number of faces, edges and vertices.
▶ Euler's rule states that: Faces + Vertices = Edges + 2.
▶ A net of a solid is a flat shape which when folded along definite lines becomes a solid. Most solids have more than one possible net.
▶ A prism is a solid with uniform cross-section.
▶ To calculate the volume of a prism, multiply the area of the cross-section by the height of the prism.

Activity

Give students the following instructions:
• Imagine a cube. Imagine it with one vertex on a flat surface and your finger holding the opposite vertex at the top so that it balances.
• Imagine a knife cutting a small slice off one vertex. What shape is the piece you have cut off? Sketch it. What shape is the new face just made?
• Cut off all the vertices with a small slice. How many pieces have been cut off? What shape is left? Try to sketch it.
• Start with a new cube and repeat your slicing, but this time cut through the mid-point of each edge when you slice. What shape are you left with?
• What is the ratio of the volume of the new solid to the old cube? What is the ratio of the volume of one of the slices to the original cube?
• Make the nets of all the solids you have worked with.

TOPIC Number sequences and mental calculations

▶ A number sequence has a starting point and a step size, for example starting at 3 and going up in 5s produces the sequence: 3, 8, 13, 18, 23, …
▶ The Fibonacci sequence is made by starting with the digits 1 and 1. Each new term is made by adding together the previous two terms.

▶ A Fibonacci-type sequence starts from any two numbers. Each new term is made by adding the previous two terms.

Activity

Give students the following instructions.

Imagine a number line stretching away on both sides of you. Find zero.

You are now going to go for walks along your number line.
- Start at 0, step on all the multiples of 3. How many steps before you pass 50?
- Start at 4, go up in sevens. Will you land on 100?
- Start at 5, go down in elevens. How many steps before you pass −100?
- Start at 9, go up in a Fibonacci sequence, how many prime numbers do you land on before you get to 100? What are they?
- Start at 7, go up in fours. As you land on each number, look at the units digit. When do they start repeating? How long is the cycle?
- Start at −5, go down in threes. As you land on each number, look at the units digit. What is the pattern?
- Start at 0. Walk along your line until you get to 10. Now fold your line around you so that 11 ends up next to 9. Look at the other pairs you have created. What is 0 next to? What is −16 next to? What do you notice about these pairs of numbers?
- Straighten the line out. Explore what happens when you fold it at different points.

TOPIC *Inverse operations*

▶ Addition is the inverse of subtraction and subtraction is the inverse of addition. Multiplication and division are inverses of each other.
▶ If you do an operation followed by its inverse, you arrive where you started from, for example $7 + 2 - 2 = 7$
▶ When you are dealing with more than one operation, you arrive where you started if you do the inverse of each operation in the opposite order, for example

$$7 \boxed{+2} \ 9 \boxed{\times 3} \ 27 \boxed{\div 3} \ 9 \boxed{-2} \ 7$$

Activity

Give students the following instructions.
- I'm thinking of a number. I multiply it by 5 and then subtract 7. The answer is 58. What number was I thinking of?
- I'm thinking of a number. I multiply it by 3. I then subtract 6. I then divide by 2 and then add 5. The answer is 23. What was my number?

Get students to discuss the strategies they used to work out the original number.

CHAPTER 3 The culture of the learner

For many students school mathematics seems completely separate from what they do at home and in the community. They cannot see the point of what they are doing in maths at school. They also cannot see the connection between the maths they do at school and the maths that they do in other places such as the market, kitchen, or the fields.

This chapter shows how to:
1 Bring the culture of the local community into the mathematics classroom.
2 Develop the idea that maths is a global activity.
3 Use the local environment to teach mathematics.

Bringing the culture of the community into the classroom is important because:
• It breaks down barriers between home and school.
• It values the mathematics that is going on in the community.
• It makes links between the mathematics that is used in the community and the school syllabus.
• It shows that the community is a good resource for mathematics.
• It makes school maths more relevant to students.

Developing the idea that maths is a global activity is important because:
• It shows that maths is not just a European activity.
• It celebrates the achievements of cultures around the world.
• It broadens students' outlooks.
• It shows where maths comes from.

Using the local environment to teach maths is important because:
• It helps students make connections between the world around them and the school.
• It helps students understand their environment.
• It helps students see how maths is used in real life.

This chapter presents activities in areas of mathematics that people use all over the world.

The topics come from these five broad areas of mathematics: counting, measuring, locating places, designing patterns and problem-solving.

Developing your own activities

Once you have tried out some of the activities in this chapter, look around for maths that is going on in your own community. Think about ways you can bring this into the classroom. Some places to look are:

- Buildings and architecture
- Weaving and cloth
- Sculptures and painting
- Weights and measures – land, groceries, cloth, fruit and vegetables, time
- Games played in the community
- Number and counting systems
- Bartering systems
- Finger counting systems

Counting

TOPIC ## Counting with different number and place value systems

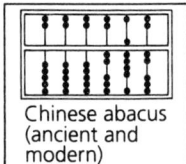

Chinese abacus (ancient and modern)	Modern Arabic
CCXCII Roman (about 100 AD)	Modern Hindi
ΣϞΒ Ancient Greek (500 BC)	Inca Quipu from Peru (1600 AD)
99 Ancient Egyptian (2000 BC)	

▶ A number system is a system of symbols that can be used in a particular way to record counting.

▶ Different systems use different symbols and are organised in different ways.

▶ Place value systems use the position of the symbols to show the value of the number. Different systems have different values for the same position of the symbol.

Activity: Which number?

The same number has been written in seven different ways.

- Work out what the number is on all seven cards.
- How many different ways can you find to write the number 23?
- Using the same symbols in each language, what other numbers can you make?
- What sums can you make?
- How do you think the abacus works?
- Can you teach someone to use it?

Activity: Arabic number square

The large square on the next page can be filled in with the Arabic numbers from 1 to 100. A few numbers have been entered. Work out how to use the numbers in the different cut-out sections to complete the large square.

Use the completed 10 × 10 Arabic number square to do the following:

- How do you write 437 using Arabic numbers?
- Choose any number, for example 210. Write it in Arabic. Use Arabic numbers in the 10 × 10 square to make up this number e.g. 100 + 70 + 40 or 75 + 75 + 60. Write all the calculations in Arabic numbers.
- Work in two teams. Each team writes 10 problems with Arabic numbers and gives them to the other team. The first team to complete the 10 problems correctly wins.

TOPIC Operating on numbers

▶ There are four operations: addition, subtraction, multiplication, division.

Activity: Egyptian multiplication

38×25 can be calculated as follows:

Step 1 Start with 1 and 38 in two columns

1	38
2	76
4	152
8	304
16	608

Double both numbers and write the answers underneath
Continue doubling the numbers and writing them down
Stop before the number in the left hand column
goes over 25

Step 2 Work out which numbers in the left column add up to 25:
$16 + 8 + 1 = 25$

Step 3 Cross out the other rows. Add the numbers in the right column to get the answer. $38 \times 25 = 950$

1	38
~~2~~	~~76~~
~~4~~	~~152~~
8	304
16	608
25	950

Make up some of your own multiplication sums using this method. Explain how it works.

Activity: Egyptian numbers

Ancient Egyptians used the following symbols: 1 for 1, ∩ for 10 and ϑ for 100

I	II	III	III I	III II	III III	III III I	III III II	III III III		∩∩	∩∩∩ ∩∩		ϑϑ ϑ
1	2	3	4	5	6	7	8	9	10	20	50	100	300

so ϑ∩∩∩ III ∩∩ III is 156   and ϑϑϑ ∩∩ III ϑ III I is 427

- Write five different numbers in ancient Egyptian symbols. The numbers can lie between 10 and 1000.
- Swap your five Egyptian numbers with those of a partner. Work out which five numbers your partner has written in ancient Egyptian symbols.
- Do the following calculations. Write the answers in Egyptian symbols.

    1.
    ∩∩∩ II
    +
    ∩∩ III
    _____

    2. ∩ III
    II
    +
    III
    III
    _____

    3. ∩∩∩ III
    ∩∩∩ III
    +
    ∩∩ III
    III
    _____

    4. Add ϑϑϑ ∩∩∩ III   and   ϑϑϑ ∩∩∩ III
            ϑϑ ∩∩∩ III   ∩∩∩ III
                ∩ II   ∩∩

    5. Take ϑϑϑ∩∩∩ III from ϑϑϑϑ ∩ I
                      II

The ancient Egyptians engraved numbers in stone tombs over 5000 years ago.

Activity: Gelosia multiplication

Gelosia multiplication uses a grid. 264 × 53 can be calculated very easily using this method.

Put the numbers 264 and 53 on a grid as shown.

Multiply 4 by 5. Write the tens part on the left hand side of the diagonal. Write the unit part on the right hand side of the diagonal, as shown.

Then multiply 4 by 3. Write the answer as explained. Complete the grid in this way.

Then add all the numbers in each diagonal strip. For example: 3 + 0 + 0 = 3. Write the sum outside the grid, as shown.

You now have the answer: 264 × 53 = 13 992.

- Try some other multiplications using this method. Note that if the diagonals add up to 10 or more, you have to carry the tens over to get the answer:
  153 × 29 → 3 13 13 7 = 4437
- Explain how the method works.
- Extend this method to multiply decimals together.

Activity: Egyptian fractions

▶ A unit fraction has a top number of 1. For example: $\frac{1}{3}$, $\frac{1}{15}$, $\frac{1}{36}$.
▶ The Egyptians only used unit fractions.
▶ The Egyptians made up $\frac{7}{20}$ by adding unit fractions:
  $\frac{7}{20} = \frac{1}{5} + \frac{1}{10} + \frac{1}{20}$
- Write the fraction $\frac{13}{40}$ as a sum of unit fractions.
- Try writing other fractions as sums of unit fractions.
- Find 3 fractions which you can write as sums of unit fractions.
- Can all fractions be written as sums of unit fractions?
- Can you find a way of adding and subtracting fractions using the Egyptian method?

TOPIC *Algebra*

▶ One part of algebra is about using symbols to stand for an unknown number.
▶ You can operate on algebraic symbols using the four rules of number.

Activity: Solving equations with Hausa numbers

- Work out the Hausa numbers from 1 to 10 by solving the equations below:
  bakwai + 6 = 13
  3 × hudu = 12
  shida − 3 = 3
  goma ÷ 5 = 2

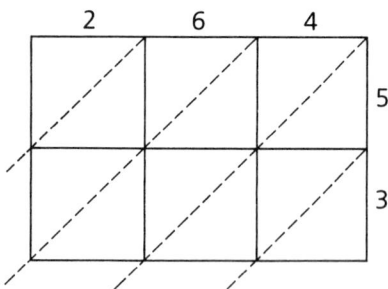

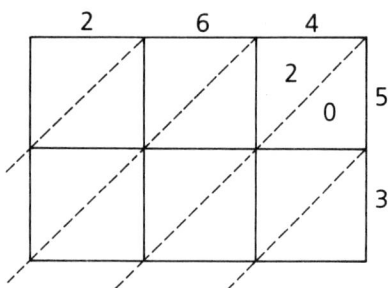

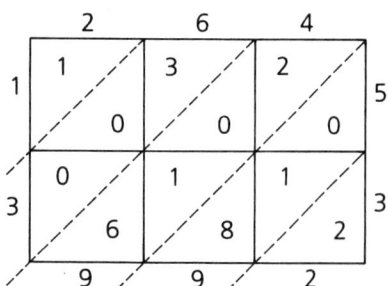

Africa

$4 \times$ biyu = 8
$(4 \times$ uku$) + 3 = 15$
$3 \times (12 -$ takwas$) = 12$
$\frac{1}{2}$ tara = $4\frac{1}{2}$
$2 \div$ daya = 2
biyar $\times$ biyar = 25

- Now answer the following in Hausa:

daya + biyu   (shida)^2
goma – biyu $\sqrt{\text{tara}} + 17$
goma $\div$ biyu   (takwas $\times$ tara) $\div$ uku
daya $\times$ uku   (goma $\times$ 10) – hudu

- Write five problems in Hausa. Give them to a partner to solve.
- Can you find out the names of numbers in another language? Write some equations and problems with these numbers. Give them to a friend to solve.

Measuring

TOPIC Measuring systems

▶ Different societies have developed their own measuring systems and measuring instruments.
▶ Early measuring systems used non-standard units such as the handspan for length, jars for volume.
▶ Standard units developed when societies with different measuring systems began to trade.
▶ The metric system is an international system with standard units of measure.

Activity: Comparing standard and non-standard units of measurement

Find out what the local traditional non-standard units of measurement are. Use them when you first start teaching measurement. You could also use them to do conversions to the metric system.

The Swahili on the East African coast used the following measuring units (given with approximate Imperial equivalents used by traders): For length:

shibiri   this is a large handspan, from the tip of the thumb to the tip of the little finger, about 9 inches.
mkono   2 shibiri – about half a yard
pima   4 mkona – about 2 yards or 1 fathom

For capacity or volume:
kibaba   this is 1 pint
kisaga   2 kibaba – 1 quart or 2 pints
pishi   2 kisaga – half a gallon or 4 pints

For weight:
wakia   1 ounce
ratli   16 wakia – 1 pound or 16 ounces
frasila   about 36 ratli or about 36 pounds

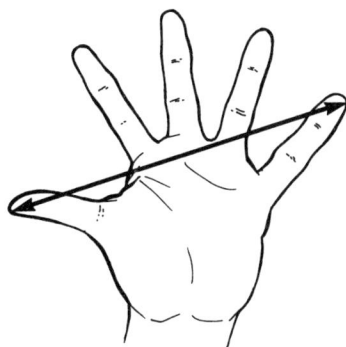
a handspan

- Estimate the measurements of different objects using the Swahili units, such as length of chalkboard in shibiri, length of room in mkono, weight of a chair in ratli.
- Measure the above objects exactly with the Swahili units.
- Discuss why these units are no longer used.
- Measure the above units exactly with metric units like cm, metre, kg.
- Find rough metric equivalents of some Swahili units, for example 1 shibiri is about 22 centimetres.

Locating

TOPIC Locating

► We can give directions or describe the position of objects using an absolute system or a relative system.
► Co-ordinates are an absolute system in maps because the origin is fixed at a longitude and latitude. Co-ordinates give the position of a point from the origin by saying how far along and how far up you have to go to get to the point.
► North, South, East, West are part of an absolute system of direction.
► Bearings are relative to the observer. Bearings give the position of a point using the angle from the North line measured clockwise and the distance from the observer.

You will need:
- *a map of your country or your district*

Activity: Using co-ordinates or bearings and distance to locate places

- Find where you are on the map. Write down your co-ordinates.
- Find places on the map you have visited or heard about. What are their co-ordinates?
- Begin with a map of the country or district or village or even with a map of the school. Choose a position on the map where a buried treasure could lie – invent the position of the treasure, but do not mark it on the map.
- Choose a starting point and write a set of instructions to help someone find the treasure. Use bearings, scale and co-ordinates in the instructions but do not use place names.

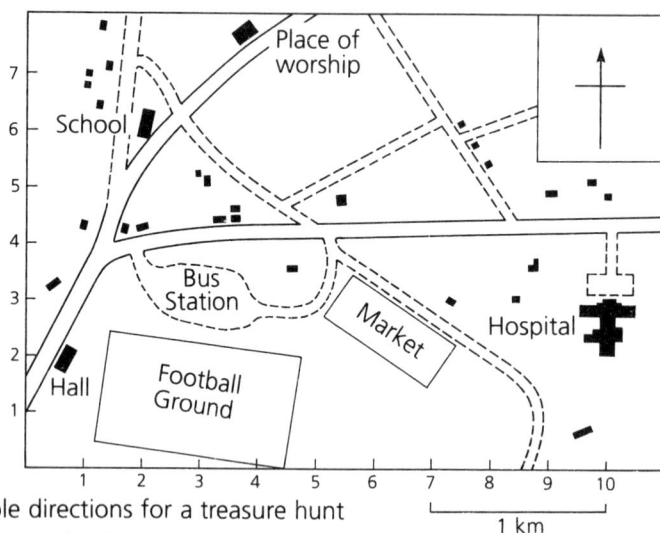

Simple directions for a treasure hunt
1. Start at (2,4).
2. Go east for 1 km, then turn 45° to the south east until you get to (8,2).
3. Turn 90° left to the north east and go 500m.
4. Half way along west side of house.
5. You will find the treasure if you look up.

Exchange journey instructions with a partner and see if they can find the place where the treasure is hidden.

TOPIC Networks

- ▶ Networks are part of topology. Topology describes the connections between points on a surface.
- ▶ The study of networks is concerned with journeys between points.
- ▶ When we can visit every point on the network without going along a previous journey, we say the network is traversable.

Activity: Networks on Shongo patterns

- Look at the first two Shongo patterns below.
  Note where the starting point of each network is. Follow the arrows to see how to draw each pattern without going along a line already drawn and without lifting your pen.

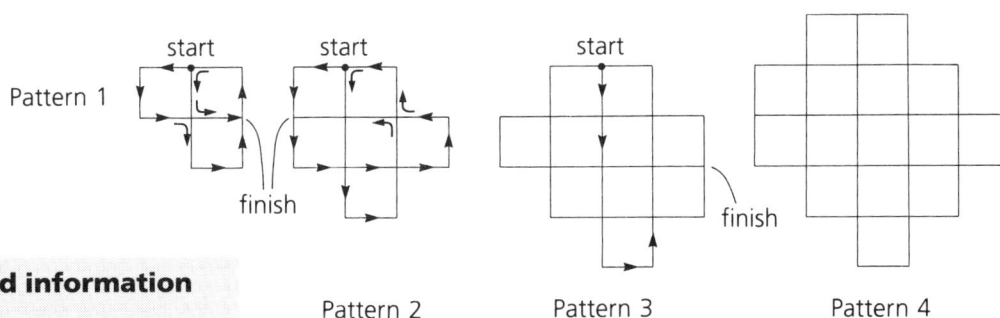

Pattern 1

Pattern 2   Pattern 3   Pattern 4

Background information

The Bakuba people of Zaïre weave Shongo patterns using raffia. Children also play games with Shongo patterns. The aim of the game is to trace a pattern without lifting the finger or going along a line already drawn.

- Try to complete the network on Pattern 3.
- Work out how to draw Pattern 4 without going over a line previously drawn and without lifting your pen. Discover the starting and finishing points.
- Investigate the number of squares in each pattern. What do you notice?
- Investigate the length of line drawn in each pattern.

TOPIC Loci

- ▶ The locus of a point is the path travelled by that point when it is moving according to a rule.
- ▶ Examples of rules for the locus of a point are:
  The point must always be the same distance from one other point, or from two other points or from a line or two lines.

Activity: Investigating loci in a fishing community

In some countries, where fish is dried by a fire, all the fish have to be the same distance from the fire.
- Work out the loci in the following problems:
  - A fisherwoman wants to dry her catch of fish. They must all be the same distance from the fire. Sketch where they would be.

– A rich fisherman has two fires. The fish must be the same distance from each fire. Sketch where they should be.

Activity: Investigating loci in an agricultural community

A goat is tied to the corner of a hut in the middle of a large field. The hut is 4 m × 6 m and the length of the rope is 9 m.
- What area of grass can the goat eat?
- What if the rope is 12 m long? What area of grass can the goat eat?
- Investigate the area of grass the goat can eat:
  - for different lengths of rope
  - for different shapes and sizes of hut
  - for more than one goat.

TOPIC *Rotation and reflection*

▶ Two ways of changing the position of a shape or object are: rotation and reflection.
▶ Rotation moves a shape through a given angle about a given point.
▶ Reflection moves a shape so that each point on the shape is the same distance on the other side of the mirror line.

Activity: Designing Rangoli patterns

Background information

Diwali or Festival of Lights is one of the main festivals of the Hindu year. During Diwali, many families decorate their homes with Rangoli patterns.

Rangoli patterns are made by repeating a design over and over again, without gaps. Rangoli patterns have many symmetrical lines through which designs are reflected.

Make a Rangoli pattern by following the six steps below.
Step 1 Begin with a square grid.
Draw in the horizontal and vertical lines of symmetry. This will divide the grid into four quarters or quadrants.
Step 2 Join some of the dots in one quadrant of the grid.
Do not draw too many lines – this will help you avoid difficulties when you reflect and repeat the design in the other quadrants.

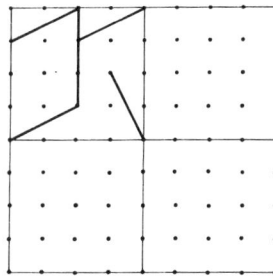
Steps 1 and 2

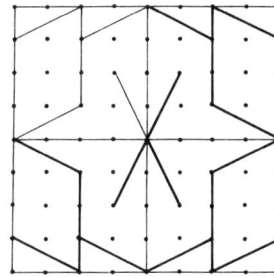
Step 3

Step 3 Reflect the lines in the first quadrant into the other three quadrants. Use the vertical and horizontal axes to reflect the lines. A small mirror can also be helpful.

Work from the first quadrant into the quadrant next to it. Then reflect both quadrants into the other half of the grid.

Step 4 Draw the two diagonals in the large original square.

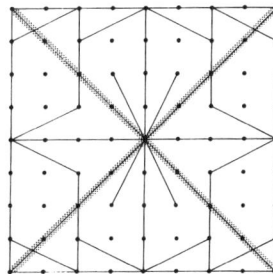
Step 4

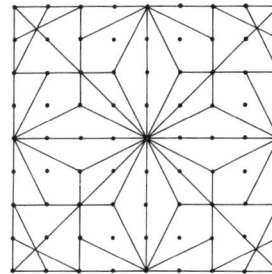
Step 5

Step 5 Reflect the lines through both diagonals. You can fold your grid along the diagonals to see where the lines are reflected. Fold the grid along one diagonal first and reflect all lines. You can place a small mirror along each diagonal instead of folding the grid.

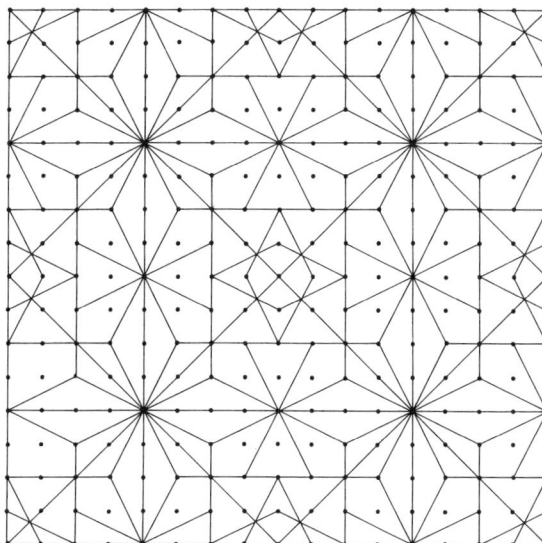
Step 6

Step 6 Now enlarge your design: add a square grid next to the first pattern you created. Repeat the design again, following steps 1 to 5. You can add more square grids and repeat the same pattern several times with no gaps and no dividing lines.

New shapes will appear. The pattern on the left developed from the five lines in step 1, repeated and reflected over and over again through different lines of symmetry.

Designing

TOPIC Designing patterns

- ▶ 2-dimensional shapes can be classified by properties like: number of sides, number of corners, length of sides, number of pairs of parallel sides, lines of symmetry.
- ▶ Some shapes fit together without any gaps to make a repeating pattern. This is called tessellation.

Background information

Islamic artists do not represent living things or people. Islamic art is based on geometric ideas and complex symmetrical patterns. Beautiful geometric patterns are found in mosques all over the world, in ancient tombs in the Middle East and on the floors of courtyards and fountains in Morocco.

Activity: Designing Islamic patterns on squares

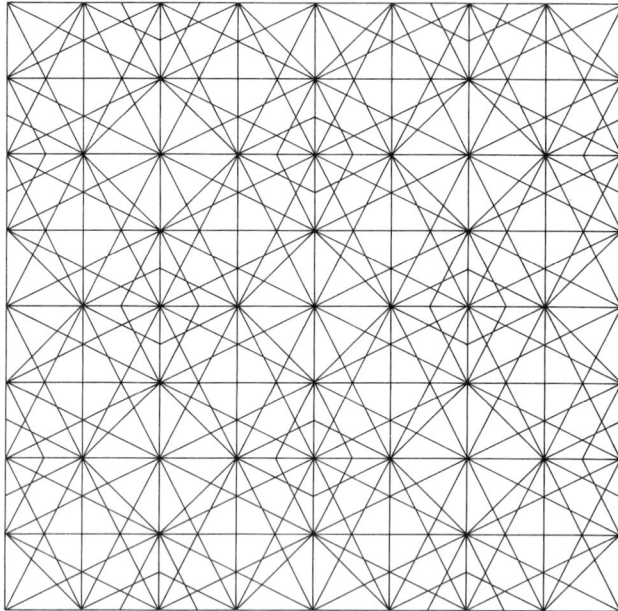

An Islamic pattern

Step 1 Draw a 5 × 5 grid (or any other size square) on square paper. Don't draw the lines too thickly as they may have to be rubbed out later.

Step 2 Draw in the vertical and horizontal midlines, as shown in the picture.

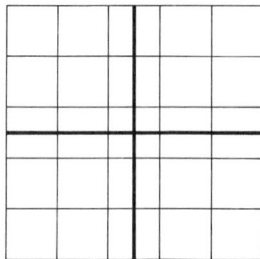

Steps 1 and 2

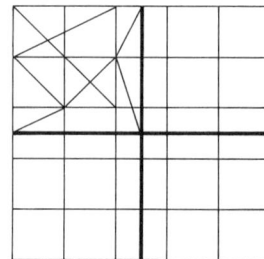

Step 3

Step 3 Draw a pattern in one quarter or quadrant of the grid.

Step 4 Reflect the lines into the other three quadrants.
Step 5 Look for interesting shapes and rub out some lines to get these. Make sure you are left with a symmetrical design.

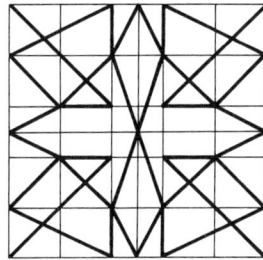 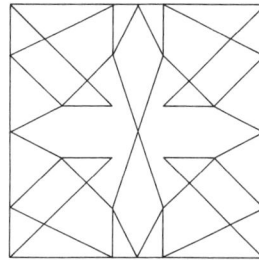 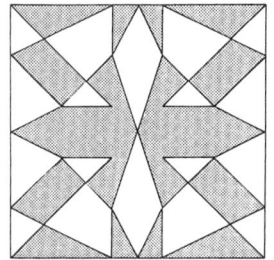

Step 4   Step 5   Step 6

Step 6 Colour in parts of the design. Keep the design symmetrical.

Extensions

- Repeat the pattern over and over, without gaps. Look for new shapes. Identify which geometric shapes occur in your pattern.
- Calculate the area of the coloured shapes in the first quadrant of the pattern. Calculate the total coloured area in the final pattern.

Activity: Designing Islamic patterns on polygons

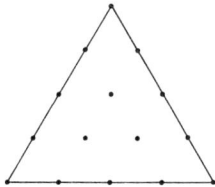

- Start with a triangle on dotty paper as shown in the picture. Draw a design inside the triangle. Put lots of triangles together and reflect the design into them.
  Rub out the sides of the original triangles. Colour in to make a symmetrical design.

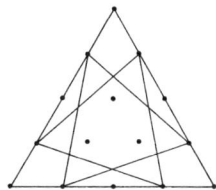 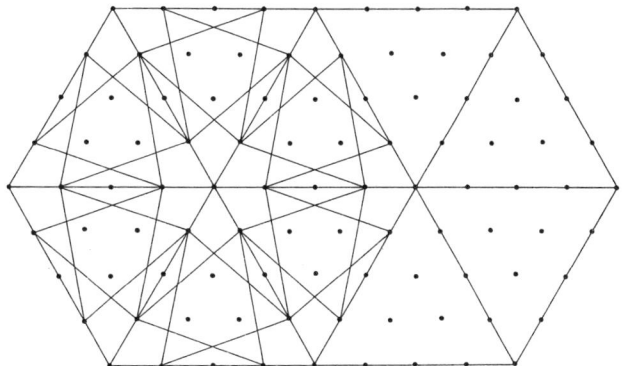

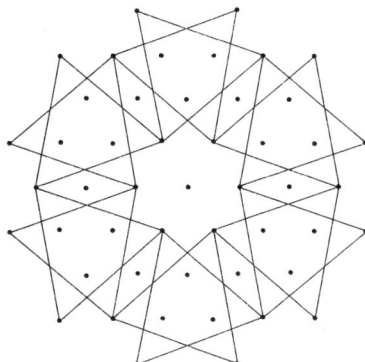 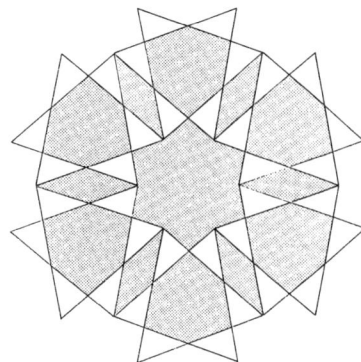

• Try with other regular shapes that tessellate, that is, they fit together without gaps.

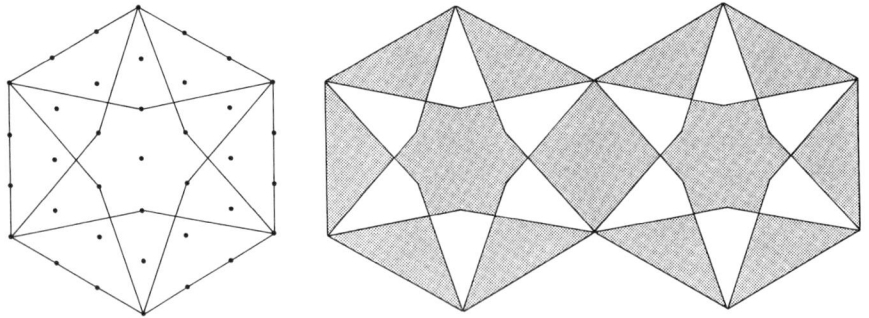

Background information

Both Buddhists and Hindus use designs specially made to help with their meditations. These are called mandalas, yantras or jantras.

Activity: Investigating Hindu and Buddhist designs

• Study the two yantras provided. Answer the questions that follow:
  – How many small triangles can you see in each?
  – How many triangles point up and how many point down?
  – How do the two yantras differ from each other?
  – Small triangles make up larger triangles of different sizes. How many of each size?
  – What other shapes do you see in the yantras? Rhombuses (diamond shapes)? Trapezia? Hexagons? Any other shapes? How many of them?
• Find yantras of your own. Look in books. Ask your religious education teachers. Ask any Hindus or Buddhists that you know.
• Try making your own yantras.

Puzzles and problems from around the world

Activity: Problems from Ancient China

1 $2\frac{1}{2}$ piculs of rice are bought for $\frac{3}{7}$ of a taiel of silver. How many piculs of rice can be bought for 9 taiels?
2 100 birds are sold for 100 shillings. The cocks are sold for 5 shillings each, the hens are sold for 3 shillings each, and the chicks for $\frac{1}{3}$ shilling. How many of each are sold? How many different answers are there?

Activity: Problems from India

1 20 people (men, women and children) earn 20 coins between them. Each man earns 3 coins, each woman earns $1\frac{1}{2}$ coins and each child $\frac{1}{2}$ coin. How many men, women and children are there?
2 3 guards were protecting an orchard. A thief met the guards one after another. To each guard he gave half the apples he had at the time and two extra. Eventually he escaped with just 1 apple. How many apples did the thief originally take?

Activity: Problems from Ancient Egypt

Background information

The Rhind papyrus was written in hieroglyphics over 3500 years ago by an Egyptian scribe called Ahmes. The papyrus was discovered by Henry Rhind in Egypt in 1858. Here are two problems included in the papyrus.

1 Seven homes each have seven cats.
The seven cats each kill seven mice.
Each of the mice would have eaten seven ears of wheat.
Each ear of wheat would have produced seven measures of flour.
How many measures of flour were saved by the cats?
2 A quantity and a quarter of it together make up 15. How much is the quantity?

Strategy games from around the world

Activity: Nine Men's Morris

This is a game for 2 players. Boards for this game have been found in Egypt, Sri Lanka and Norway.

You will need:
- 9 counters in one colour for Player 1
- 9 counters in another colour for Player 2
- a board (see next page)

Rules
- Players take it in turns to place one counter each on the black dots on the board until players have all nine counters on the board.
- Players take turns to move one counter at a time to an empty dot on the board. Counters can only move along a line in any direction but no jumping over occupied dots is allowed.
- When a player gets three counters in a row, they remove one of their opponent's counters.
- If a player is reduced to two counters and cannot move, they have lost the game.

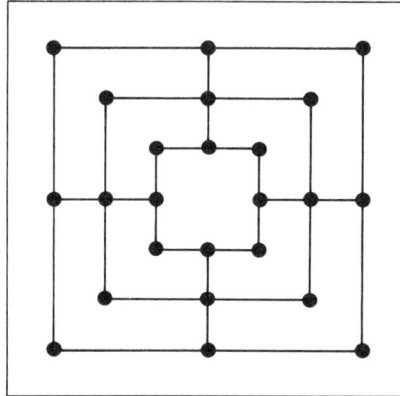
Board for Nine Men's Morris

Play the game several times and then discuss the following questions:
• Is there a 'best' opening move?
• How many positions are possible after one move by each player?
• What is the maximum number of counters which can be on the board without making a row?
• An ant starts anywhere on the board and walks along all the lines. What is the shortest possible route?

Activity: Congklak

A game for 2 players.

There are many variations on this game. It is played in many countries.

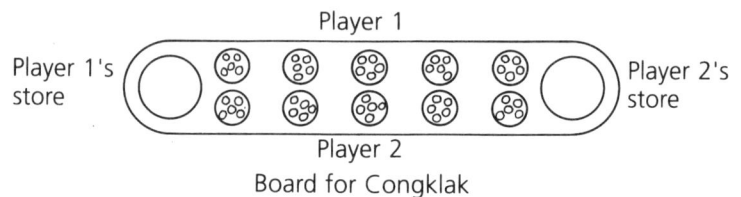
Board for Congklak

• Use 25 stones for Player 1.
• And 25 shells for Player 2.

Rules
• To play, five shells, stones or seeds should be placed in each of the 10 holes, but not in the stores.
• Player 1 and Player 2 take turns to pick up the counters, and go around the board clockwise, 'sowing' one counter into each hole, including their own store, but not their opponent's store. The player with the most counters in their store at the end of the game is the winner.
• To start, one player lifts the counters from any hole on their side of the board and sows them, one at a time, into holes, going clockwise around the board. A counter is dropped into the player's own store but not into the opponent's.

You will need:
• *a rectangular board with 2 parallel rows of 5 holes and 2 larger stores, one at each end*
• *50 counters: you can use shells, stones or seeds*

The last counter of a turn:
- If the last counter falls in any loaded hole, the counters are lifted from that hole and the sowing continues.
- If the last counter falls in an empty hole on the opponent's side, the turn ends and the opponent plays.
- If the last counter falls in an empty hole on the player's side, then the counters in the opponent's hole opposite are captured and put in the player's store. The opponent then plays.
- If the last counter lands in the player's store, the turn ends and the opponent plays.
- The game ends when one player has no counters left on their side; the opponent then adds any counters left on the board to their own store.
- The winner is the player with more counters in their store at the end of the game.

Activity: Cows and leopards

A game for two from Sri Lanka

Rules
- Player 1 has 2 counters of the same colour. These are the leopards. Player 2 has 24 counters of a different colour. These are the cows.
- Player 1 starts by placing 1 leopard on any spot on the board. Player 2 then places 1 cow on any spot on the board.
- Player 1 places the second leopard, followed by Player 2 who places another cow.
- Cows and leopards can only move one spot per turn along straight lines in any direction.

You will need:
- *2 counters of one colour*
- *24 counters of another colour (use beads or bottle tops)*
- *a board, as shown*

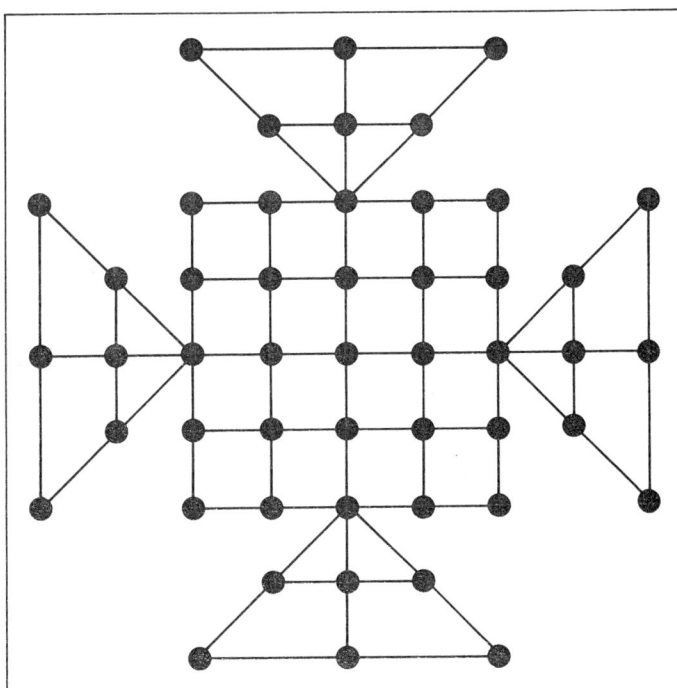

The board for Cows and Leopards

- Player 1 can begin to move a leopard, one spot per turn. Player 2 will continue to add 1 cow per turn. Only when all 24 cows are on the board can Player 2 begin to move cows, one spot per turn.
- A leopard can kill a cow by jumping over it along a straight line onto an empty space. Leopards usually start to kill cows before all the cows are on the board. Cows cannot kill leopards but can trap them by preventing them from moving.
- To win, the leopards must kill all the cows, or the cows must prevent both leopards from moving.

CHAPTER 4 Mathematics and second language learners

Learning mathematics is a challenge for many students. When mathematics lessons are not in the language which students know best, the challenge of learning mathematics is even greater.

In order to learn mathematics well, students need to use a lot of language. They need to listen to the teacher talking, presenting and explaining. They need to read their textbooks and worksheets. And they need to ask questions and discuss their ideas to improve their understanding of mathematical concepts.

It is therefore important for teachers to help students learn mathematics in a second language as well as to help them understand the way that language is used in the textbook and examination papers.

It is often said that mathematics teachers are language teachers. Mathematics teachers need to think about teaching the language of mathematics as well as mathematical ideas and skills.

This chapter will help you use language in the mathematics classroom in a way which will develop students' ability to learn mathematics. In this chapter, we look at ways to:
- develop students' understanding by providing them with opportunities to talk about mathematics
- help students learn mathematics by listening in English
- help students to understand their textbooks
- write clear worksheets for students.

Ways to support maths learning in a second language

Learning mathematics always involves a lot of language. When students are learning in a second language, the role of language (both mother tongue and second language) is even more important.

How can teachers help students to learn mathematics through a second language? What is the role of the students' first language in the mathematics classroom?

You need to think about the use of the students' mother tongue in the classroom. Some countries do not allow the use of the mother tongue in the classroom, others encourage it.

In our view, the aim of mathematics classes is to help students learn mathematics. Using their mother tongue can help students when they cannot get to grips with mathematical ideas in English.

If the school policy allows the mother tongue to be used in the classroom, there are many ways to use it to help students learn mathematics (and English!). Some of the activities below show how the mother tongue can be used to help students learn mathematics.

Groups based on language ability

- Students who share a language can work together in order to talk about a difficult task or clarify new mathematical ideas in their first language
- A student whose English is not very strong can do pair work activities with a student who is more fluent in English.
- Students who do not speak the same mother tongue can do pair work activities on familiar topics so that they have to talk in English about the mathematical ideas they understand well.
- Problems and new ideas can be presented in English, followed by pair work in the mother tongue. Then whole class discussion and checking of the problem can be in English.

Activity: Learning the key words and phrases of a new topic

Key words for quadratic equations:
re-arrange
brackets
substitute
common factor
collect like terms
factorise

- Prepare a sheet of key words and phrases for students. It must list all the important words you will use when you introduce and explain a new topic like how to factorise and solve quadratic equations. Give the sheet out to students before you start your explanation. As the students hear the key word or phrase they tick it on their sheet.
- When students have understood the new topic or method introduced, they can do the following activities to help their English:
  - If the key words are not in order on the sheet, put them in the order you will use them to do the new mathematics, for example factorise and solve a quadratic equation
  - Write definitions or give examples of the key words and phrases in English
  - For key words that continue to cause difficulty, write a definition or explanation in your mother tongue.

Speaking and listening

Students' understanding of mathematics can develop and improve if they have lots of opportunities to talk about mathematics, for example by discussing concepts, solving problems aloud, describing mathematical processes to each other, explaining ideas to other students.

Discussion with the teacher and with other students is a valuable way to learn and improve maths. Through discussion and talking students learn to:

- express their own ideas
- explain mathematics to other students
- make sense of other people's ideas
- challenge other people's ideas
- clarify their own thinking
- argue for their own ideas and convince others
- improve their understanding
- build confidence.

Many students spend a lot of their time listening to the teacher. Although the teacher may be very skilful at explaining things to the whole class, some students may not understand. And students are often too shy to ask for help, so teachers do not always know when students need help. Also, many students do understand but cannot always answer questions or show they understand.

How often do teachers say:

I know she understands but she cannot put it into words.

When students get opportunities to talk and discuss in the mathematics classroom, it helps them learn. It also helps the teacher. By listening to students talking, teachers can discover what they understand and where they need help.

Ways to encourage students to talk about mathematics

Activity: Back-to-back

- Two students sit back-to-back. One student has a diagram or a model which he describes to the other student. The other student draws the diagram or makes the model without seeing the original. The student drawing cannot ask questions. The student with the diagram must give clear and correct instructions so that the other student produces a good copy of the original diagram or model.
- Sit back-to-back. Each student has 4 or 5 matchboxes. One student must arrange her matchboxes into a shape. The other student has to make the same shape by asking questions. For example:
  - Are any matchboxes lying on their side?
  - Are any matchboxes placed on top of each other?
  - Do the matchboxes form a regular shape such as a rectangle? a circle?

The aim is to make the shape by asking as few questions as possible.

Only yes/no questions are allowed, that is the questions can only be answered with a yes or no.

- One member of a group goes to look at an arrangement of matchboxes made by another student. Then she returns to the group who all ask her yes/no questions until they can arrange the matchboxes correctly.

Activity: Discussing questions from the teacher in pairs

Start or finish a lesson with this quick activity to get students thinking and talking. Give students a question or statement to discuss with a partner for 2–3 minutes. For example:

- What is a circle?
- The answer is 10. What are the questions?
- What quadrilaterals can you see in this room?

Give questions related to the topic of the lesson.

Activity: Agree/disagree with statements about trigonometry

Work in pairs or threes. Take it in turns to read statements about trigonometry. Discuss each statement and decide if you agree or disagree with it. Give your reasons for agreeing or disagreeing. Correct any statements that are false.

Sample statements about trigonometry for discussion:

True   False

1 The hypotenuse is the longest side of a right-angled triangle.

2 $Tan = \dfrac{opposite}{hypotenuse}$

3 The sine of an angle is always greater than zero.

4 The adjacent side is next to the angle.

5 $Cosine = \dfrac{adjacent}{hypotenuse}$

6 Sine, cosine and tangent can be used to calculate the sides and angles of any triangle.

7 Tangent is a measure of the gradient of a line.

8 "SOHCAHTOA" was a Japanese football player.

Activity: Giving explanations

- Work in pairs and explain the following to each other:
  - A student says that $2(a + b)$ is the same as $2a + b$. Explain what his mistake is.
  - Explain how to construct a right-angled triangle.
  - Explain how to solve the equation $2x + 7 = x + 11$.
- Mark your homework in pairs. When your partner has a mistake in a problem that you did correctly, explain how to do the problem correctly.

Activity: Conflict discussion

Choose some ideas that many students often misunderstand. Write them down as statements on pieces of paper. Give to each pair or small group of students one statement to discuss as in the example below.

Decide if each statement below is always true, sometimes true or never true. Explain your answer or give examples. Convince members of the group that you are right.

- Multiplying a number always makes it bigger.
- $a - b = b - a$.
- Squaring a number makes it bigger.
- Numbers cannot have more than five factors.
- To multiply by 10, add a 0.
- Multiplying by $\frac{1}{2}$ is the same as dividing by 2.

Sets of statements about many mathematical topics are possible, for example shape, probability, trigonometry, percentages.

Activity: Information sharing

- Prepare some sets of cards with one or two statements on each card so that when a set of cards is put together, it will describe the whole problem. Divide the class into groups. The number of students in each group must be equal to the number of cards in a set.
- Deal out a set of cards to each group (one card per student).
- Give each group the instruction:
  Construct a geometric figure with all the properties on the cards.
- Each card should have one statement. Statements for the cards:
  - Both pairs of opposite angles are equal
  - Both pairs of opposite sides are equal
  - The diagonals do not intersect at right angles
  - All the angles are not equal
  - The diagonals are not equal
  - Both pairs of opposite sides are parallel
  - The diagonals bisect each other
  - There are no lines of symmetry

Read your card but do not show it to other people in the group. Solve the problem above together.

Zogian food

- Prepare a set of 25 cards with the statements given on page 76. Students can solve the problem given below in groups of 5.

You will be given some information about feeding the Zogians. Deal the 25 cards out amongst your group. You may share the information on your cards with other people in the group, but you may not show them your cards. As a group, work out the answer to the question below:

How many fields do you need to feed the Zogian community for a week?

Statements for the cards:

- 2 burgs of seed yield 12 burgs of grain.
- 6 burgs of grain yield 30 loaves.
- There are 1700 adult women in the Zogian community.
- There are 500 priests in the Zogian community.
- There are 600 girls in the Zogian community.
- There are 1500 adult men in the Zogian community.
- There are 500 boys in the Zogian community.
- Children eat $\frac{1}{2}$ a loaf a day each.
- Priests eat $1\frac{1}{2}$ loaves a day each.
- Adult women eat 1 loaf a day each.
- Adult men eat $\frac{3}{4}$ of a loaf a day each.
- There are 12 days in a Zogian week.
- Adult men do not work in the fields.
- Priests oversee the planting of the seed.
- The crop is harvested on Muliday.
- Zogian fields are 7 oxteds wide.
- Zogian fields are 13 oxteds long.
- The number 7 has religious significance.
- 33 burgs of seed can be planted in a Zogian field.
- 1 bag of fertiliser covers 91 square oxteds.
- There are 14 kells in a burg.
- It takes an adult woman $2\frac{1}{2}$ days to plant a field.
- It takes 3 Zogian umbers to yield a crop from seed.
- Girls spread the fertiliser over the seed.
- It takes 2 girls 3 days to fertilise 7 fields.

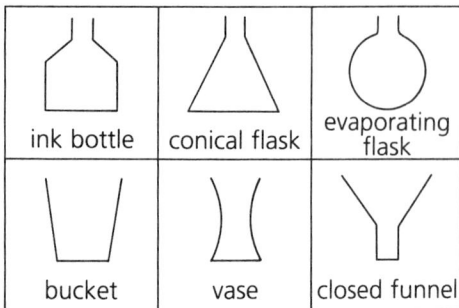

ink bottle	conical flask	evaporating flask
bucket	vase	closed funnel

Activity: Interpreting graphs

All the containers on the left are filled with water from a tap. The water flows at a constant rate.

Six of the graphs below show the rate at which the containers fill up with water. Each graph shows the height of the water along the vertical axis and the time taken to reach that height along the horizontal axis.

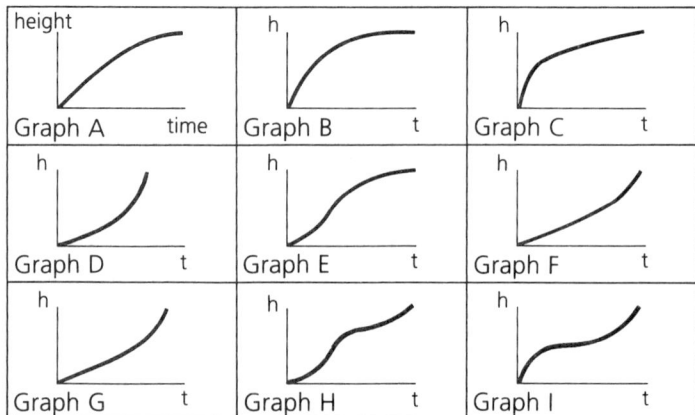

- Look at the containers and the graphs above.
  Decide which graph represents which container and match each container with its graph.
  Sketch the container for the remaining three graphs.
  Draw another container. Ask another student to sketch the graph that shows the rate at which the container fills with water.
- Extend the activity by writing rationale cards which give reasons why each graph matches with one container. This helps students learn the language necessary to discuss the graphs.
- Students invent their own bottles and graphs to go with them. Collect these and mix them up. Get students to match graphs and containers as above.

Activity: Mini lessons

This is a very good way to revise for examinations. Each student in the class chooses a topic from the syllabus that they are good at. Make sure that each student chooses a different topic.

Each student prepares a short lesson on the chosen topic with examples.

Students take it in turns to give a mini lesson on a topic to small groups of students who find the topic difficult.

Understanding textbooks

Teachers need to help students use and understand the textbook they have – both the mathematics and the English.

There are three kinds of vocabulary in mathematics textbooks:
- technical or subject specific, like cosine, parabola, rational number, square root
- semi-technical, like elevation, depression, construct, calculate
- common words not specific to maths such as train timetable, money, interest, hire purchase

The activities below will help students understand these different kinds of vocabulary used in mathematics.

Activity: Build a dictionary of mathematical words

A dictionary can be made on a set of cards or in a book.
Use one card per word and store the cards alphabetically.
Or use one page per letter of the alphabet if you are using a book.
- As you read your textbook or listen to teacher explanations, collect together words which have a similar meaning. Collect words in English and your mother tongue. Write all the English words with a similar meaning on a card or page of the book. On the opposite page you can write the words with the same meaning in your mother tongue.

sum	solve
add	work out
put together	get the answer
addition	evaluate
plus	find
+	calculate
	express

- When you come across a mathematical word you don't understand, see if it is defined in the class dictionary. If not, add it to the dictionary with a definition or example or diagram to illustrate it.

Dictionary entries are best when they include a simple written statement and a picture or example, as in the second definition below. Try to avoid long and complex definitions, like the first definition below.

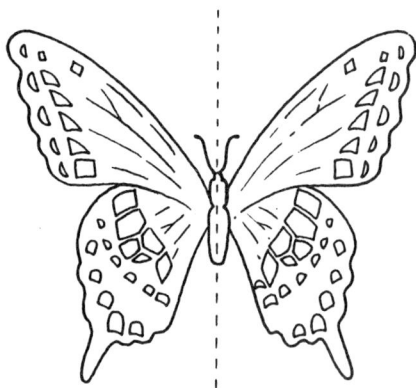

> SYM-ME-TRY/'SImatrI/n[u]
> (beauty resulting from the) right correspondence of parts (in size, design etc.) between parts.
> 'The bump on the left side of her head spoilt the symmetry of her face.'

> Symmetry
> A picture which is balanced has symmetry.
> If you cut a picture in half, both halves are the same – the halves are symmetrical.

- Keep the dictionary in a special place in the classroom. Add to the dictionary each time you find another new word or another word which means the same thing as a set of words in the dictionary.

Activity: Identify mathematical words that have a non-mathematical meaning

Certain mathematical words have a different meaning in everyday speech, like root, face, odd.

Build a list of all words like this, with simple explanations or examples of their mathematical meaning.

If you have difficulties with apparently familiar words when you read your textbook, especially word problems, check whether the word causing the difficulty has a special meaning in mathematics.

Common words with special meaning in maths
root, as in $\sqrt{4}$; find the square root.
odd, as in odd numbers; 1, 3, 5, …

Activity: Understanding the vocabulary of word problems

Word problems ask you to apply mathematical solutions to problems in the real world. Many of the words in these problems are not specific to mathematics.

Divide the class into groups of 3–4 students. Each group will look at 3–4 word problems from the textbook. In this way, the whole class can analyse over 50 word problems.

- Make a list of the words you do not understand in your set of word problems.
- Copy the list. Keep this copy.
- Exchange your list with another group's list. Compare your list of words with the other list. On your list, tick any word that the other group identified.
- Circulate all the lists in this way. Each group will compare their list with all the other lists. Tick a word on your list every time it appears on the list of another group.
- Choose the 5–10 words most commonly identified. These are words that appear in word problems regularly but that many students do not understand.
- Find the meaning of these words and enter them in the class mathematics dictionary.

Teachers also need to go through past exam papers and make lists of the vocabulary which causes problems for students. Make sure students understand the meanings of these words, especially when they are preparing for exams.

The following section is for teachers only. The activities are for teachers to do, individually, at in-service training workshops or with the other mathematics teachers at the school.
We begin by looking at a few different mathematics textbooks in order to understand:
- how different textbooks use language and present mathematics.
- What difficulties students may face when they read textbooks.

Then we will look at how to write worksheets that are clear and easy to understand.

Activity for teachers: Reading textbooks in a foreign language (1)

In this activity you will read extracts from a textbook in a language you do not understand. This will help you imagine what some students experience when they read a textbook in English.

- Try and answer the question below:
  1004 Utfor overslagrakning ocn svara med heital.
  a) 3,56 . 7,2 b) 10,6 . 3,3 c) 5,9 . 9,7

- What do you think the question is asking you to do?
- On what do you base your judgements?

- What kind of difficulties will students have when they try to do the problems above?
- What do the dots and commas mean? What does 1004 refer to?
- Besides the words (which are Swedish), how would you re-write the question to make it less confusing?
- Look at the question and the cartoon below:

Utfor overslagrakning ocn svara med heital.
a) 3,56 . 7,2   b) 10,6 . 3,3   c) 5,9 . 9,7

- What clues are there to the nature of the mathematics you are being asked to do?
- Does the cartoon help you understand the activity? If so, how?
- What do you need to understand in order to answer the questions?

The second version of the same problem shows how pictures and a few words can be used to help you understand. You could now probably answer question 1004 in Swedish. The repeated use of sentence patterns in the cartoon helps you understand the question and solve the problem. You may be able to copy the model sentence patterns to help you answer the question in Swedish.

Remember that when students misinterpret a question or answer it incorrectly, the problem may not be caused by their mathematical knowledge. The problem may be caused by a lack of understanding of the textbook or by a badly written textbook!

Activity for teachers: Reading textbooks in a foreign language (2)

Try to answer the three questions below.
- Which problems can you do? What helps you do this problem?
- Which problems are impossible to even begin? Why?
- Did the pictures help you? Why/why not?

Arter
Får en miljon gula artor plats 1 klassrummet?

Hur stor låda behover du till en miljon artor?

Struten

Sex olika smaker av glass finns 1 kiosken.

På hur många olika satt kan du valja din glass-strut med tre kulcr?

Snigeln

En snigel kryper upp på insidan av en brunn.
Varje dag kryper den upp 3 meter.
På natten glider den ner 2 meter.
Hur många dagar tar det innan den når brunnens kant?

The extract above shows that:

- Pictures do not necessarily help. They need to describe the problem rather than just look attractive.
- The amount of text is not necessarily important. It is the pattern of the words which helps us understand the meaning.
- Sentences providing information before the question are helpful. A question followed by information or another question is less helpful.
- Numbers are easier to read if they are written as symbols such as 4, rather than as words like four.

Activity for teachers: Reading textbooks in a foreign language (3)

The extract below is from a textbook in Nepal. Answer the questions on the right.

- What do you think the lesson is about? How do you know?
- Translate the table of numbers. How did you do this?
- Make a similar table for another number, for example 2.

The Nepali extract shows several things:

- When trying to work out the numbers, we often assume we must use the base 10 system.
- We can use the patterns in the table of numbers to translate the numbers.
- The picture of children walking in lines of 4 provides a big clue to understanding the table. How could the picture have been made more helpful?

Activity for teachers: Study the textbook

Study the textbook you use with students:
- How are questions numbered?
- How are exercises numbered?
- Do the illustrations help understanding or are they only for entertainment?
- What difficulties do your students have with the textbook? How can you help them?

Study the vocabulary of the textbook:
- Which words are likely to cause problems for your students?
- Which kinds of words will you need to help students with:
  - technical words like cosine, parabola
  - semi-technical words like elevation, construct
  - common words not specific to maths such as tariff, hire purchase.
- Develop ways of helping students with these different kinds of words.

Activity for teachers: How do students read charts, diagrams and tables?

Students may find it difficult to read charts, diagrams and tables. They may find the conventions of reading across and down very difficult or confusing. They may not know what keys mean and they may not understand abbreviations.

Look at the charts and tables in the textbook you use. Choose one good table or chart and one weak table.
- Discuss what makes a good table or chart.
- Discuss what each table or chart shows. How will you help students read the table or chart?

Select three difficult geometric diagrams:
- How will you help students understand these diagrams?

Activity for teachers: Writing clear worksheets

Compare the following two versions of the same question. Find as many differences as you can. Make a list of do's and don'ts for writing maths problems.

Two girls share three pounds pocket money with the younger girl getting less than the older. What percentage of the total pocket money does the younger girl receive if they share the money in the ratio 2:3? How much money does the younger girl receive? How much does the older girl get?

Two girls share £3. Shazir gets less money than Sufia. They get the money in the ratio 2:3.

a. What percentage of the money does Shazir get?
b. How much money does Shazir get?
c. How much money does Sufia get?

Guidelines for writing worksheets

Presentation

Make sure that the text is clear, easy to read and well-spaced.

Use pictures to reinforce ideas and concepts and to make reading easier. Pictures should be clear and relevant to the text. Place pictures near the relevant part of the text.

Sentences

- Use short sentences. Very long ones are more difficult to understand. Aim for one idea or piece of information in each sentence.
- Separate information from questions. Write a clear statement followed by a clear question.
- Do not ask several questions in one sentence. Write them as separate questions.

Grammar

- The passive voice is difficult so try to use the active. For example:
  'Change the decimal to a fraction'
  is easier to understand than:
  'The decimal should be changed to a fraction'.
- Keep sentences with 'if' short. Try to break the sentence down into two or more sentences.
- Present information in the correct sequence. For example:
  'The train took 10 minutes to reach the station after the stop for 15 minutes.'
  It is better to write:
  'The train stopped for 15 minutes. It then took 10 minutes to reach the station.'
- Avoid complicated descriptions with many adjectives. A lot of this language is unnecessary and can be very confusing.

Vocabulary

- Use simple vocabulary where possible.
- Choose the easiest word when you have a choice, for example 'need' rather than 'require'.
- Use technical words which students will meet in the exam.
- Be consistent in the use of technical words. For example use 'minus', 'take away' or 'subtract', but not all three on the same worksheet.

CHAPTER 5

Planning for learning

In this chapter, we draw together the ideas about teaching methods, resources, culture and language described in the previous chapters. We describe how they can be used in planning your teaching.

We look at two kinds of teaching plans:
- a course plan for the whole syllabus
- a scheme of work for topic areas.

What is a course plan?

A course plan shows all the topics that must be covered during the course of a year. A course plan will show:
- The titles of the topics to be taught.
- The order of the topics.
- The amount of time to spend on each topic.
- The timing of revision, exams and tests.

How to write a course plan

In some countries, the course plan is provided by the Ministry. In others it is not. If it is provided by the Ministry, you can go straight to the section on the scheme of work on page 85.

1 Identify all topics to be taught

Collect all the information provided by the Ministry. This may include: a syllabus, textbooks, past examination papers and other advice and guidance notes. Read all this material and discuss it with your colleagues. Find out what the aims and objectives of the course are. Try and get a good idea of what is expected. Write a list of all the topics to be taught during the course.

2 Assess students' knowledge

Find out what students have done before they start the course:
- What topics have they covered?
- What topics have they done a little bit of?
- What topics are new to them?

Make notes on your list of topics.

3 Make a calendar of the school year

Find out how much time is available for getting through the course:
- How many maths lessons are there each week? How long do they last?
- How many weeks are there for the whole course?
- How many weeks are used by exams, public holidays, sports days, speech days etc?
- When are the holidays?

Draw up a plan showing the time available to teach the course. Show the number of terms. On your plan for each term show how many teaching weeks there are, when the holidays, exams, public holidays etc. are.

4 Order the topics

Decide the order in which you will teach the topics:
- Which topics should be taught early on because they cover basic skills necessary for later topics?
- Are some topics easier than other topics?
- Are some topics best taught during particular seasons of the year?
- Are some topics best taught together because they are closely linked?
- Is it best to have a variety of topics in a term?
- What is the order of topics in the textbook? Do you have to follow it?

Cut up your list of topics and put them in order.

5 Plan time required for each topic

Decide how long you need to spend on each topic. Make sure you have enough time to cover the syllabus:
- Can you spend less time on easier topics?
- Analyse past examination papers. Which topics are tested most often in the exam? Which topics carry the most marks in the exam?
- Write down how much time to spend on each topic.
- Put the topics on your course plan. Discuss your plan with your colleagues.

What is a scheme of work?

A scheme of work is much more detailed than a course plan.
A scheme of work shows how each topic will be dealt with.

For each topic, a scheme of work gives:
- the title of the topic and the amount of time to be spent on it.
- aims and objectives for teaching the topic. The objectives are in order of increasing difficulty.
- the teaching methods that will be used to meet the aims and objectives.
- activities to teach each objective.
- a list of teaching resources for each objective.
- references to exercises in the textbook for each objective.
- homework.
- assessments.

How to write a scheme of work

In some countries, the scheme of work is provided by the Ministry. In others it is not. If it is provided by the Ministry, use that as the basis for your teaching and add your activity ideas to it.

1 Identify the aims and objectives for the topic

Decide what the aims and objectives of the topic are.

An aim describes in general terms what students must learn and what they must be able to do at the end of studying the topic. Objectives describe the smaller steps that students must achieve in order to meet each aim.
- Read the syllabus, advice and guidance from the Ministry.
- Look at the textbook chapter on the topic.
- Look at exam questions on the topic. What must pupils be able to do in the exam?
- What knowledge, skills and understanding do pupils need to have acquired by the end of this topic?
- Can the knowledge, skills and understanding be put in order of difficulty?
- Make a list of the aims of the topic. Make a list of objectives for each aim of the topic. Put both lists in order of difficulty.

2 Plan activities for each objective

For each objective, decide what activities students need to do in order to achieve the objective:
- When you are choosing activities, you will need to think about including a variety of teaching methods: exposition by the teacher, investigation, problems and puzzles, games, discussion, practical work and consolidation and practice. The scheme should include a broad balance of types of activity.
- Go through your textbooks, teaching aids and other books. Collect together all the activities you can find which teach the topic. Choose a range of activities to include in your scheme of work. You can add to these as you discover more activities.
- Try to vary classroom organisation. Give students opportunities to

experience whole class teaching, groupwork (mixed ability, streamed or friendship groups), pair work and individual work.

3 Collect the necessary resources

Decide what resources you need to teach the topic. Think about:
- what resources are available locally
- what resources you will have to make
- what resources are available within the school.

Collect together all the resources and teaching aids you need to teach the topic. Make a note of them in your scheme of work.

4 Use the textbook for consolidation and practice

Decide what exercises in which textbooks can be used for practice and consolidation of the topic. Think about:
- levels of difficulty
- which skills are being practised
- grading exercises, if necessary
- the number of textbooks in the class
- are there enough exercises in the textbook?

Note in your scheme of work which exercises you will use for each objective. You can add to this as you find other exercises in different textbooks.

5 Plan homework

Decide how many homeworks you will set during the topic. Think about:
- How long should each homework last?
- Can students take textbooks home? Do you have to write worksheets? Do you have to write the homework on the chalkboard for students to copy down?
- What is the purpose of each homework? Is it to practise skills learned in class, to collect data, to revise or memorise new formulae etc?

Plan all the homeworks for the topic and write them into the scheme of work.

6 Plan how to assess and test students

Decide how you are going to find out how much students have learned about the topic. Think about the kind of assessment you will use, such as:
- written tests
- mental tests
- homework
- question and answer sessions during the topic
- when will you do the different kinds of tests?

- how you will mark classroom work and homework?
- how you will use past exam questions?

Write any tests that are needed. Collect together past exam questions. Include these in the scheme of work.

···

A sample scheme: three-dimensional solids

This scheme of work approaches the topic through discussion, practical work, games and investigations. Explanation and presentation by the teacher can be used after students have had opportunities to develop their understanding by other methods.

Aims

Students will learn to:

1 use a variety of different representations of 3-D solids such as isometric drawings, nets, solids.
2 explore 3-D solids through drawing and practical work using a range of materials.
3 visualise, describe and draw 3-D solids.
4 construct 3-D solids from a variety of materials and from given information.

Objectives

Students will be able to:

1 use everyday language to describe 3-D solids.
2 use mathematical names to identify common 3-D solids and describe their properties (faces, edges, vertices).
3 classify 3-D solids in a variety of ways, including the use of Euler's rule.
4 make 3-D solids from a variety of materials by linking given faces or edges.
5 construct 3-D solids by accurate drawing and measuring.

Resources

- equilateral triangles and squares
- matchboxes or cubes
- set of 3-D solids
- a bag to hold the solids (Obj. 1)
- set of playing cards (Obj. 2)
- cardboard equilateral triangles and squares (Obj. 3)
- graph paper or squared paper
- isometric paper

Activity: Feely bag

Language activity
Pair work

A and B sit back-to-back. A has a bag with different solid shapes in it.

A feels the shapes in the bag but does not look at them. Then A describes what he can feel to B. A must not use the names of the shapes.

B must try and draw it.

Swap.

Activity

Language activity
Pair work

A and B sit back-to-back.

Each person has 6 cubes or matchboxes.

A makes a solid shape with the cubes or matchboxes and keeps it hidden from B. A describes the shape to B.

B has to try and make the solid shape.

Swap so that B makes a shape and describes it to A.

Some words you might use:

straight	bottom
long	left
short	right
edge	below
corner	under
end	over
top	beside

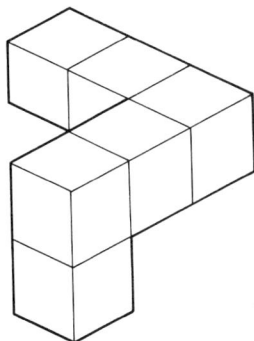

Activity

Language activity
Pair work

You will need a collection of irregular solid shapes.

Work in pairs, A and B.

Put out the shapes on the table between A and B.

A looks at a solid shape and describes it to B without pointing. B has to point to the shape she thinks A is describing.

Swap.

Activity: Card game

Game
Individual, pair work or threes

You will need a set of cards, like the ones shown on page 90. Work individually, in pairs or threes:

- Match each picture of a solid shape with its name and set of properties.
- Give a definition of 9 solid shapes.
- A has the cards with the pictures. B has the cards with the properties. C has the cards with the names.
  B begins by placing one card with a set of properties on the table. A and C must put the matching card down. The one who does so first wins the set of three cards.
- In pairs, play Snap with two sets of cards.
  See page 14 for instructions for Snap.

6 faces - all squares 8 vertices 12 edges	2 faces - 1 circle 1 sector 1 vertex 1 edge	1 face 0 edges 0 vertices

5 faces - 2 triangles
    3 rectangles
6 vertices
9 edges
	6 faces - 2 squares
	    4 rectangles
	8 vertices
	12 edges
		3 faces - 2 circles
		    1 rectangle
		0 vertices
		2 edges

4 faces - equilateral
    triangles
4 vertices
6 edges
	5 faces - 1 square
	    4 triangles
	5 vertices
	8 edges
		8 faces - 2 hexagons
		    6 rectangles
		12 vertices
		18 edges

cube	cone	sphere
cylinder	cuboid	triangular prism
tetrahedron	square based pyramid	hexagonal prism

Activity

Investigation
Individual

- For each solid below, record its name, the number of faces, the number of vertices and the number of edges. Put your results into a table and see if you can discover any rules.

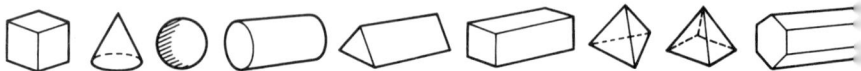

Name	Faces	Vertices	Edges

Objectives 3 and 4

Activity: Making polyhedra

Practical work
Individuals

You will need cut-out equilateral triangles and squares with sides of equal length.

Make some polyhedra using only the triangles. For each polyhedron, record:

- the number of triangles you use

- the number of vertices
- the number of edges.

Look for patterns in your results.

Make some polyhedra using only the squares. For each polyhedron, record:
- the number of squares you use
- the number of vertices
- the number of edges

Look for patterns in your results.

Teacher explanation and presentation of Euler's rule may be helpful here for students who do not see the patterns in the last few activities.

Euler's rule states:
  No. of faces + no. of vertices = no. of edges + 2.

Activity: Making and investigating polyhedra

Practical work and investigation
Individual or pair work

Make some polyhedra using squares and triangles. For each polyhedron record:
- the number of triangles and squares you use
- the number of vertices
- the number of edges.

Look for patterns in your results. Use graphs to show your results, as in the example given.

Can you find any patterns?

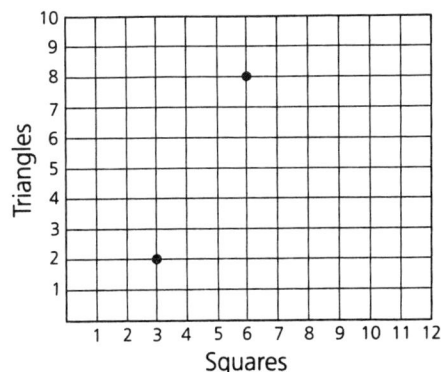

Number of squares and triangles for different polyhedra

Objective 3

Activity: Classifying polyhedra

A regular polyhedron has:
- regular polygons for its faces
- all its faces the same
- all its corners look the same.

Which of the shapes you made are regular polyhedra?

Objective 4

Activity

Investigation
Individual

- Here is one net of a tetrahedron.

  - Find all the different nets for a tetrahedron.
  - Record them.
  - How many different ways can you find to put tabs on the nets?

- Here is one net of a regular octahedron.
  - Find all the different nets for an octahedron.
  - Which nets are symmetrical?
  - How many different nets are there?
  - How do you know when you have found them all?

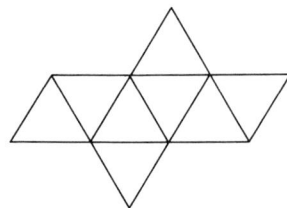

Objective 5

Activity

Practical work and investigation
Individual

You have a piece of cardboard or paper 64 cm by 52 cm.
- Make or draw as many cubes with sides 5 cm long as you can:
  - Think about all the different nets of a cube.
  - Think how you can fit them together with few gaps.
  - Don't forget the flaps!
- Repeat with regular tetrahedrons with sides 5 cm long.

For further activities, refer to activities that use matchboxes on pages 44–5.

Homework 1

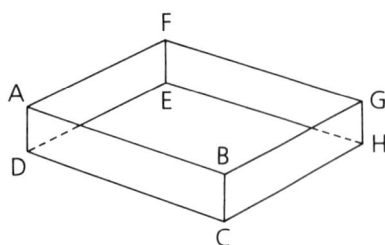

1 Look at the diagram.
  a Along which edge do faces AFGB and AFED meet?
  b Along which edge do faces BGHC and ABCD meet?
  c Which edges meet at vertex E?
  d Which edges meet at vertex G?
  e Which edges meet at vertex D?
  f At which vertex do edges EF and AF meet?
  g Which faces meet at edge DE?

2 Look at the diagram.
  Which faces or edges intersect at:
  a vertex C?
  b edge ED?
  c vertex F?
  d edge AE?
  Where do the following intersect:
  e face ACB and face BCDF?
  f face EDF and face ACDE?

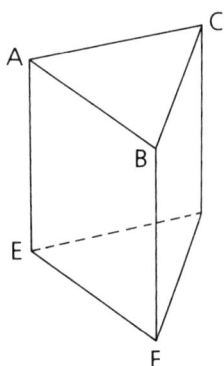

3 Draw a square-based pyramid. Label the vertices A, B, C, D, and E. Make up some questions about where faces, edges and vertices meet. Write your answers separately.

Homework 2

1 List as many everyday examples as you can of:
  a spheres
  b cones
2 Draw as many different prisms as you can. For each one, write down the number of faces, edges and vertices.

3 Accurately draw on card the nets of two solids: one prism and one pyramid. Remember the flaps! Cut out your nets and make up your solids.

Assessment

1 I have four faces and four vertices. What am I? Draw me and my net.
2 I have one face and no vertices. What am I?
3 I have six vertices and ten edges. Five of my faces are triangles. What am I? Draw me and my net.
4 Write down the names of six different solids.
5 Draw an accurate construction of the net of a hexagonal prism with all edges 4 cm long.
6 Sketch these solids on isometric paper:
   a cube
   b cuboid
   c tetrahedron
   d square-based pyramid.

....

Sample scheme:
Forming and solving linear equations

This scheme of work approaches linear equations through investigations and problem-solving. In this way, students have the chance to develop their own methods and rules for solving linear equations. Teacher explanation and presentation can be done after students have had the chance to develop their own methods. Then practice and consolidation can follow when they know the rules and methods of solving equations.

Aims

Students will learn to:
1 use letters to represent variables.
2 construct, interpret and evaluate formulae, given in words and symbols, related to mathematics, other subjects or real-life situations.
3 solve linear equations, using the best method for each problem.

Objectives

Students will be able to:
1 construct and interpret simple formulae expressed in words.
2 evaluate simple formulae expressed in words.
3 construct and interpret simple formulae expressed in symbols.
4 evaluate simple formulae expressed in symbols.
5 formulate and solve linear equations with whole number coefficients.

Objectives 3–5

*Investigation
Whole class*

Activity: Number pyramids

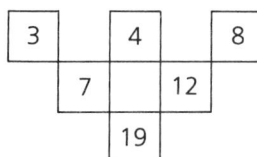

* Study the relationships between the numbers in the pyramid below. Write down as many equations as you can that show the relationship between the numbers in the pyramid. What do you notice about the numbers in the different layers of the pyramid?

- Fill in the missing numbers in the pyramids below. Use the same patterns between numbers that you found in the pyramid above.

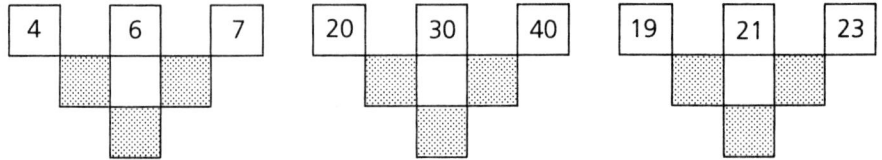

| 4 | | 6 | | 7 | | 20 | | 30 | | 40 | | 19 | | 21 | | 23 |

- Now make up your own number pyramids for your neighbour to complete.
- Fill in the missing numbers in the pyramids below. Then find the value of the letter in each pyramid that makes the bottom number in the pyramid correct. Show exactly what you do to find the value of the letter.

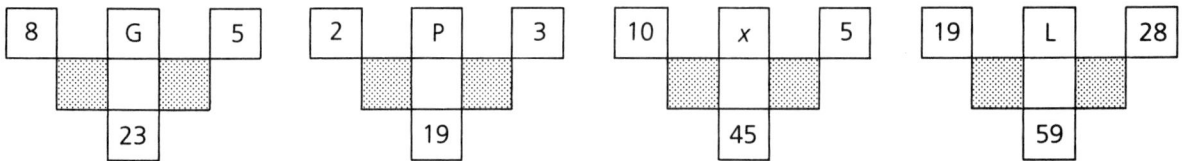

| 8 | | G | | 5 |
| | 23 | |

| 2 | | P | | 3 |
| | 19 | |

| 10 | | x | | 5 |
| | 45 | |

| 19 | | L | | 28 |
| | 59 | |

- Make up some of your own number pyramids as follows:
  - Fill in the whole pyramid with numbers. You can also use negative numbers or fractions in the top row.
  - Copy the pyramid, but leave out all the numbers in the middle rows.
  - Change one of the top numbers to a letter.
  Give your pyramid to your neighbour to complete.
- Now complete the pyramids below, filling in the shaded squares. Then find the value of x in both pyramids below.

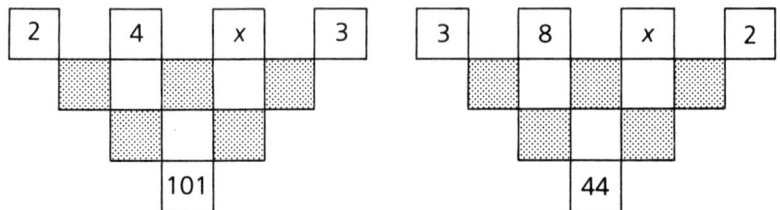

| 2 | | 4 | | x | | 3 |
| | | 101 | |

| 3 | | 8 | | x | | 2 |
| | | 44 | |

- Make up your own number pyramids with four levels, as above. Use the same method you used before. Give your pyramid to your neighbour to solve.

Objectives 1–5

Activity: Piles of stones

Problem-solving
Individual work

- You have 3 piles of stones. The second pile has 3 times as many stones as the first pile. The third pile has 2 stones less than the first pile. There are 78 stones altogether.
  How many stones in each pile?
- The first pile has 4 times as many stones as the second pile. The

third pile has 3 stones less than the first pile. There are 69 stones altogether.

How many stones in each pile?

- Check your answers with someone else. Do you agree?
- Make up some problems of your own for your partner to solve.

Objectives 1–5

Activity: Problem-solving

Practice and consolidation
Individual work

1 Three people aged 15, 18 and 20 were in a broken-down car with a monkey and a box of 275 oranges. They agreed that the oldest person should have 5 more oranges than the youngest, and that the middle one should have 3 more than the youngest. They gave the monkey 6 and then divided the rest. How many did each get?

2 A delivery van is to take 200 sacks of potatoes to 3 villages. The first village is to have 20 sacks more than the third village and the second village is to have twice as many sacks as the first village. How many sacks are delivered to each village?

3 A farmer has 600 sacks of beans to sell to four families. He decides to sell the same number to the first two families, 40 more than this to the third family and 80 more than the first two to the fourth family. How many sacks does each family get?

4 In an election 41 783 votes were cast for the candidates of the three main political parties. The winning candidate received 8311 more votes than the candidate who came second. The winner also received 5 times as many votes as the candidate who came third. How many votes did each candidate receive?

5 There were four candidates in an election, placed first to fourth. The fourth candidate received 3040 fewer votes than the third and the second candidate received 5255 more than the third. The winner received twice as many votes as the fourth. It was discovered that the number of votes received by the winner and the fourth candidate together was the same as the number of votes received by the other two candidates. How many votes did each candidate receive?

Objectives 1–5

Activity: Solve the following equations

Practice and consolidation
Individual work

1 $2x + 3 = 15$
2 $6x = 7$
3 $\frac{4x}{5} = -2$
4 $\frac{5x}{6} = \frac{1}{4}$
5 $-3x = 1$
6 $10 = 2 - x$

1 $-2x = x + 12$
2 $a - 3 = 3a - 7$
3 $-2x = 2x - 7$
4 $-x - 4 = -3$

5 $-x = -5$

6 $\frac{x}{10} = -\frac{1}{5} - \frac{x}{5}$

1 $2(3x - 1) = 3(x - 1)$

2 $-2x = 3(2 - x)$

3 $7x = 3x - (x + 20)$

4 $-(x + 1) = 9 - (2x - 1)$

5 $3y + 7 + 3(y - 1) = 2(2y + 6)$

6 $5(2x - 1) - 2(x - 2) = 7 + 4x$

1 The sum of three consecutive numbers is 276. Find the numbers.

2 The sum of four consecutive numbers is 90. Find the numbers.

3 I'm thinking of a number. I double it, then add 13. I get 38. What is my number?

4 The sum of two numbers is 50. The second number is 4 times the first. Find the two numbers.

5 The length of a rectangle is twice the width. The perimeter is 24 cm. Find the width.

6 The width of a rectangle is $\frac{1}{3}$ of the length. If the perimeter is 96 cm, find the width.

Objective 5

Activity: Form and solve equations

Find the size of all the unknown angles.

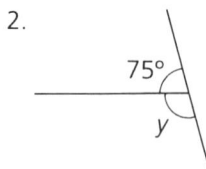

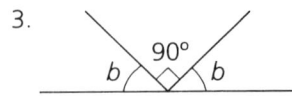

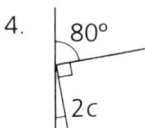

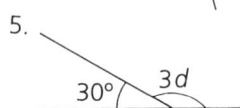

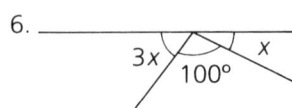

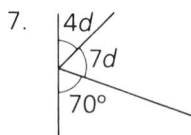

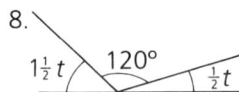

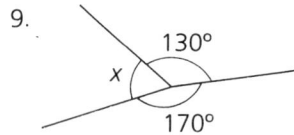

Homework

Form and solve equations for the following problems.

1 There are boys and girls in a class of 32. There are 6 more girls than boys. How many girls are in the class?

2 Ashraf is 4 years older than Elene. Their total age is 46. How old is Ashraf?

3 Anna is 3 times older than Christina. Their total age is 24. How old are they?

It may be helpful to summarise, explain or present what students have been doing in the activities so far. Teacher explanation and presentation on forming and solving simple linear equations is necessary for those students who did not develop successful methods to solve equations.

4 There are 21 pieces of fruit in a bag. There are twice as many mangoes as bananas. How many of each type of fruit?

5 There are two numbered doors. The numbers differ by five. They add up to 41. What are the numbers on the doors?

6 The Choi family has 4 more children than the Chang family. Altogether there are 8 children. How many children in each family?

7 There are 64 children on Bus A and Bus B. There are 7 times more children on Bus A than on Bus B. How many children on each bus?

8 I am thinking of a number. I double it and add 7. I have now got the number 19. What did I start with?·

Assessment

1 Put numbers in the boxes to make the equations true.

    a $\square + 7 = 51$ **b** $100 - \square = 42$

    c $9 \times \square = 162$ **d** $\dfrac{\square}{13} = 18$

    e $\square + 11 < 29$ **f** $\square^2 = 121$

2 Marie started with a number x. She doubled it and then added 7. Her answer was 23. Form and solve an equation to find what number Marie started with.

3 Hanif is Lusca's son. Lusca is 6 times as old as Hanif. By the time Hanif is 18, Lusca will be 8 times as old as Hanif is now. How old is Lusca?

4 Mary asked her grandmother how old she was. She replied, 'In 7 years' time, I shall be 3 times as old as I was when I got married.' Mary's grandmother then told her she had been married for 41 years.

    a Taking her age now to be y years, write down an equation involving y.

    b How old is Mary's grandmother?

5 Solve the following equations:

    a $3(x - 2) = 18$

    b $4(x + 3) = 48$

    c $3p + 7 = 5p - 13$

    d $2a = -6$

    e $3(b + 4) = -24$

    f $5(c + 3) = 12 - c$

CHAPTER 6 Getting going

This chapter will help you to use new ideas and methods in your teaching. Developing as a maths teacher can be an exciting and stimulating process. It can be both challenging and rewarding.

You can use a wide range of activities to get going:

- try out new teaching ideas with students
- try out new resources
- make teaching aids and resources – one set per month or term
- try out teaching aids and resources
- talk to colleagues and share ideas
- talk to students – find out what they like and dislike about maths classes
- evaluate your practice
- read books, magazines and information from the Ministry about teaching mathematics
- go on courses and workshops, if possible
- improve your own mathematics
- team-teach with a colleague
- observe other colleagues
- write and review schemes of work and lesson plans
- find out what maths is going on in the community
- explore the environment for mathematical ideas
- write your own worksheets
- invent your own games and puzzles
- plan investigations
- start a maths club
- organise your classroom
- write assessments
- join a National Maths association
- contact local curriculum development agencies, teacher training colleges, etc.

There seems to be a lot to do! The question is 'Where to start?'

In your classroom

There is no right answer to the question, 'Where to start?' You could choose one, or some, of the ideas from the list above and start there. But it is best to start with something you are interested in.

The diagram on the next page shows one way to start developing and enriching your teaching.

Start
↓
Choose a topic from the scheme of work

Build activity or method into scheme of work

Find suggestions from this book and other sources of information for activities

Discuss with colleagues, maths associations, curriculum development unit

Develop an activity for the classroom

Getting going

Try the activity yourself

Revise activity, if necessary

Try out the activity with a small group of students

Assess how effective the activity was in enabling students to learn

Adapt the activity if necessary

Teach the lesson using the activity

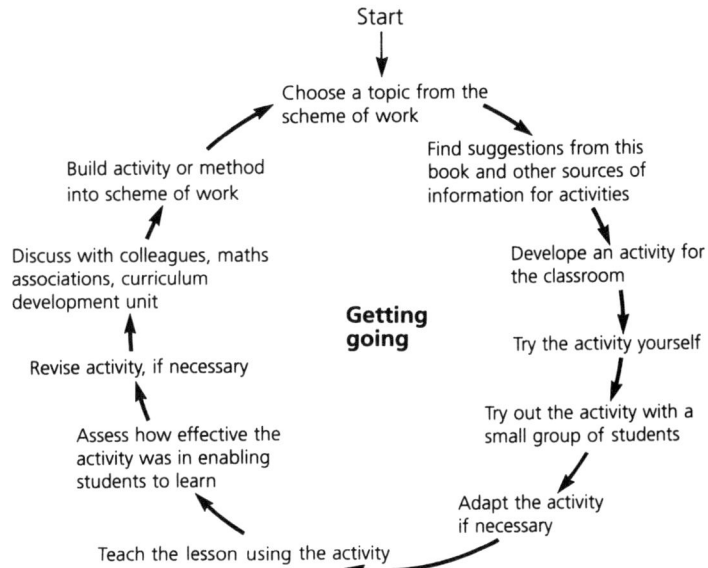

In your school

If you are in a position to co-ordinate mathematics teaching in your school, you will want to improve standards of teaching and learning in the school as a whole. It is important to have a plan to help everyone work together. We suggest that you create working groups of teachers to:

- Develop a syllabus for all students in each year group. Refer to Ministry guidelines. Include a list of all content and skills to be taught. Work out topics and modules within topics.
- Create a curriculum map to show the timing of the school year and when each module/topic of mathematics is to be taught (see page 84).
- Develop a scheme of work for each module/topic. Include teaching methods and activities, resources and assessment tasks (see page 86).
- Develop a wide range of challenging and varied activities to teach each topic.
- Try out activities in the classroom.
- Develop a range of assessment techniques to find out about students' learning.

- Share and evaluate outcomes.
- Build successful activities into schemes of work.
- Share successes with other colleagues.

Getting going is a never-ending cycle. The more you raise standards, the more you will want to achieve. We hope this book has helped you start.

Glossary of terms

Algebra The study of mathematical properties and relationships and their representation using general symbols such as letters of the alphabet.
Example: $y = 4x - 2$
If $a = 10$, $b = 6$, $c = -2$, find the value of $\frac{ab}{c}$.

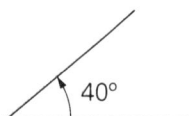

Angle Amount of turn, usually in degrees.

Arithmetic progression A sequence of numbers in which each number is larger (or smaller) than the preceding number by a constant amount.
Example: 2, 4, 6, 8, 10…

Axis Reference line from which co-ordinates are measured.

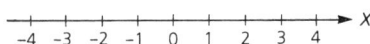

(axes) More than one axis.

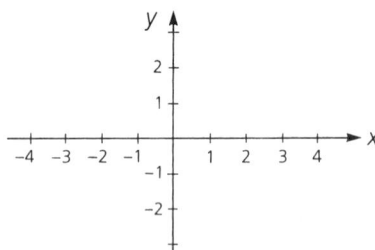

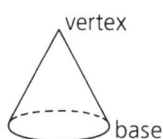

Base Bottom of a shape or solid.

Base (number base) The number size of the group used in counting.

Bearing The angle measured clockwise from North to the object. The bearing is measured in degrees.

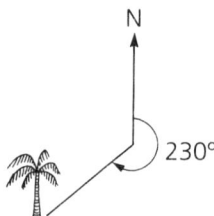

Capacity The measure of the amount something can hold.
Example: A 1 litre bottle

Classify Sort objects according to their properties.

Combining Putting together.
Example: Adding, tessellating

Comparative measurement Identifying the size by comparing with an agreed standard or unit.
Example: 1 teacup = 100 ml

Comparing Looking for similarities or differences.

Complex Uncommon or irregular shapes; something which is not simple.

Congruence The property of being identical in every respect.

Example: congruent triangles

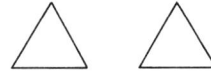

Congruent Identical in every respect.

Co-ordinates A set of numbers which fix points in space.
Example: (2, 3)

Cuboid A solid which has rectangles for all of its faces. A rectangular prism.

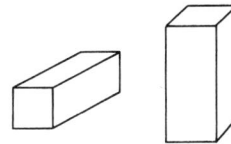

Data A collection of information on a subject.

Database A way of storing data.

Decimal fraction A fraction whose denominator is a power of ten. Usually written using a decimal point.
Example: $\frac{19}{100}$ = 0.19

Diagonal A straight line drawn from one vertex of a polygon to another vertex (not a vertex next to the first one).

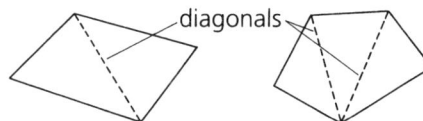

diagonals

Die Usually a cube (commonly made of wood, bone or plastic) with 1 to 6 dots on each face. Dots on opposite faces add up to 7. Dice can also be other solids, such as an octahedron, with 1 to 8 dots on the faces.

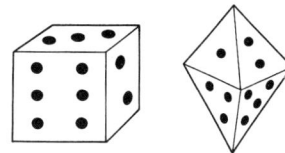

Dimension The number of co-ordinates required to represent a line, shape or solid:
a line is one-dimensional
a shape is two-dimensional
a solid is three-dimensional.

Enlargement A transformation where an object becomes larger or smaller by a constant scale.

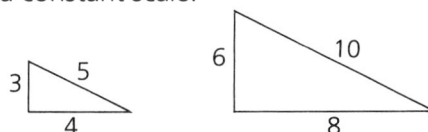

3 5 4   6 10 8

Equivalence Having equal value.
Example: $2x = 10$

Experimental outcomes The actual recorded results of experiments.

Factor A quantity which divides exactly into a given quantity.
Example: $3 \times 4 = 12$, so 3 and 4 are factors of 12

Fibonacci sequence A number sequence. Each number is made by adding the two numbers before it.
Example: 0, 1, 1, 2, 3, 5, 8, 13...

Fraction The ratio between the number of parts into which an object can be partitioned and the number of those parts taken.
Example: $\frac{4}{7}, \frac{8}{11}, \frac{12}{100}$

Function The rules which define a mapping.
Example: $n \rightarrow n + 2$

Geometric progression A sequence in which each number after the first number is the product of the preceding number and a fixed number.
Example: 1, 2, 4, 8, 16, 32...

Horizontal Parallel to the earth's skyline or horizon:

Hypothesis A statement made to explain a set of facts and to form the basis for further investigation.
Example: 13-year-old girls run faster than 13-year-old boys.

Inequality A statement which says one quantity is greater than or smaller than another.
Example: $x > 4$, $y < 7$

Interpreting Drawing conclusions from data.

Inverse The operation which reverses a previous operation.
Example: Addition is the inverse of subtraction

Irrational numbers A number which cannot be expressed as a fraction.
Example: $\sqrt{2}$, π

Isometric drawing A type of drawing which shows all three planes of a solid object.

Likelihood The probability that something will happen or not.

Line A line segment is the shortest distance between two points. A straight line is the extension of a line segment in both directions.

Mapping The action of relating elements in one set to elements in another set according to given rules.
Example: ×10
      $1 \rightarrow 10$
      $2 \rightarrow 20$
      $3 \rightarrow 30$

Mathematical pattern A pattern which has a starting point and which develops according to one clear rule.

Example: 0.01, 0.1, 1, 10, 100

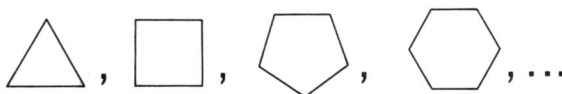

△ , □ , ⬠ , ⬡ , ...

Multiple A number made up of two or more factors other than 1.
Example: The multiples of 3 are the numbers in the 3-times tables, going on forever: 3, 6, 9, 12, 15...
multiples of 5: 5, 10, 15, 20...

Negative Less than zero.
Example: −4, $-\frac{1}{10}$

Net A plane shape which when folded along definite lines becomes a solid.

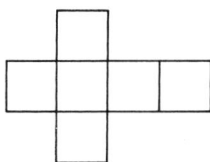

one net of a cube

Number sequence A set of numbers placed in order according to a rule.
Example: Rule: ×2 then −1
Sequence: 2, 3, 5, 9, 17...

Operation The action of combining or partitioning.
Example: addition, subtraction, multiplication, division

Ordering A system of arranging things in relation to each other or in a sequence.

Ordinal A number which indicates a position in a sequence.
Example: 1st, 2nd, 3rd, 4th...

Pattern An arrangement of things according to a rule.
Example:
```
2    4    6    8   10
     4    8   12   16   20
          8   16   24   32   40
```

Percentage A fraction written as part of one hundred.
Example: 41% or $\frac{41}{100}$

Perimeter The boundary of any plane shape: the length of this boundary.

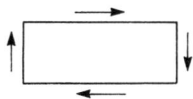

Perpendicular At right angles to a line or plane.

90°

Pi or π The ratio of the circumference of a circle to its diameter.

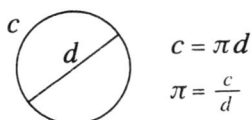

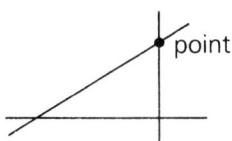

$c = \pi d$

$\pi = \frac{c}{d}$

Plane A flat surface. A line joining any two points on the plane lies completely within that surface.

point

Point A dot on a plane which has a position but no size.

Polygon A shape with many straight sides.

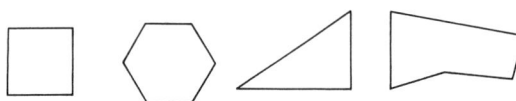

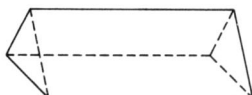

Polyhedron A three dimensional closed shape which is bounded by many plane faces.

Power The number of times you multiply a thing by itself: the result of doing this.
Example: $3 \times 3 \times 3 \times 3 = 3^4$

Prime number Numbers which have only two factors, 1 and the number itself.
Example: 1; 3; 5; 7; 11

Probability The measurement of the likelihood of something happening.

Properties The ways in which things behave and the qualities they possess.
Example: Some properties of a square:
- 4 straight equal sides
- 4 right angles
- diagonals are equal
- diagonals bisect each other at right angles.

Proportional Maintaining a constant ratio irrespective of quantities.

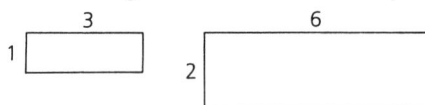

Ratio Two or more quantities of the same kind compared one to the other.
Example:

Ratio of black beads to white is 3:1

Rational number Number which can be written as the ratio of two whole numbers.
Example: -12, 8, $\frac{6}{13}$

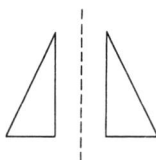

Reflection A transformation resulting in one or more images.

Regular Having all side lengths and interior angles the same.

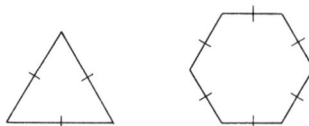

Rotation A transformation where a shape is turned about a fixed point on a plane.

Scale The relationship between a length on a map or graph and the actual length it represents.

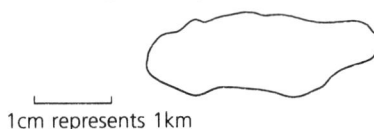

1cm represents 1km

Sequence A set of numbers, terms and so on placed in a certain order.
Example: 1, 2, 4, 8, 16…

Series A collection of terms which are separated by plus or minus signs where each term is usually related to the previous term by a rule.
Example: 1 + 2 + 4 + 8 + 16 +…

Shape A closed region.

Similar Having corresponding angles the same and corresponding sides proportional.

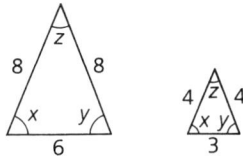

Speed Rate of change of distance with respect to time.
Example: 50 km per hour

Square number Produced by multiplying any number by itself.
Example: 1 × 1   2 × 2   3 × 3
1^2 2^2 3^2

Square root The factor of a number which, when squared, gives that number.
Example: $\sqrt{100} = 10$

Statistical average The three commonly used statistical averages are mean, median and mode.

Standard Internationally recognised unit of comparative measure.
Example: metre, ml, kg, hour, m^2

Symmetry Exact matching of points of any object relative to dividing point, line or plane

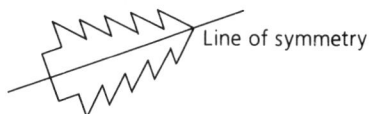

Line of symmetry

Term A number, letter or item which is found in a series.

Tessellating Combining shapes to fill the plane.

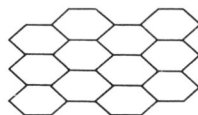

Theoretical probability A numerical measure of how likely an event is to occur on a scale of 0–1, where 0 is impossible and 1 is certain.

Transformation A mapping which relates one point to its image.
Example: Translation, reflection, rotation, enlargement

Translation A transformation where every point in a shape moves the same distance in one direction.

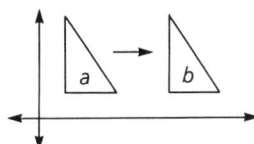

Turn To move round a point, to change direction by moving through part of a circle.

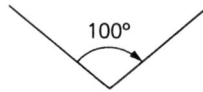

100°

Uncertainty The amount of unpredictability.

Vertical At right angles to the horizontal.

Volume The amount of space an object occupies.

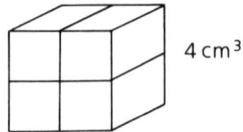

4 cm³

VSO Books

VSO Books is the publishing unit of Voluntary Service Overseas. More than 21,000 skilled volunteers have worked alongside national colleagues in over 59 countries throughout the developing world since 1958. VSO Books draws upon this range of experience to produce publications which aim to be of direct, practical use in development. Care is taken to present each area of volunteer experience in the context of current thinking about development.

A wide readership will find VSO Books publications useful, ranging from development workers, project implementers and teachers to project planners, policy-makers and ministry officials in both the South and the North.

Information from VSO Books can also be found on the World Wide Web: http://www.oneworld.org/vso/

Other books in the VSO/ Heinemann Teachers' Guide series

How to Make and Use Visual Aids by Nicola Baird and Nicola Harford, 128pp, paperback, VSO/Heinemann, ISBN 0 435 92317 X

This highly illustrated practical manual shows how to make a wide range of visual aids quickly and easily, using low cost materials which are simple to find or improvise anywhere in the world. Teachers, teacher trainers and development workers will find it indispensable.

The Science Teachers' Handbook by Andy Byers, Ann Childs, Chris Lainé, 128pp, paperback, VSO/ Heinemann, ISBN 0 435 92302 1

The Science Teachers' Handbook is full of exciting and practical ideas for demonstrating science in even the lowest-resourced classroom. VSO teachers and their colleagues from around the world have developed these ideas to bring science to life using local resources and creativity.

Setting Up and Running a School Library by Nicola Baird, 138pp, paperback, VSO/Heinemann, ISBN 0 435 923048

This lively and practical guide makes running a school library easy and fun. This book has been written especially for non-librarians and because it is based on the work of VSO teachers and their colleagues in low-resource situations, it takes into account the reality of schools in developing countries. Even with few resources it is possible to set up a school library which will make a real difference.

Current VSO Books publications include:

Adult Literacy – A handbook for development workers by Paul Fordham, Deryn Holland and Juliet Millican, 170pp, paperback, VSO/Oxfam Publications, ISBN 0 85598 315 9

Agriculture and Natural Resources – A manual for development workers by Penelope Amerena, 117pp, hardback looseleaf, VSO, ISBN 0 9509050 3 8

Care and Safe Use of Hospital Equipment by Muriel Skeet and David Fear, 188pp, spiral bound, VSO Books, ISBN 0 9509050 5 4

Culture, Cash and Housing – Community and tradition in low-income housing by Maurice Mitchell and Andy Bevan, 134pp, paperback, VSO/ITP, ISBN 1 85339 153 O

Introductory Technology – A resource book by Adrian Owens, 134pp, paperback, VSO/ITP, ISBN 1 85339 064 X

Made in Africa – Learning from carpentry hand-tool projects by Janet Leek, Andrew Scott and Matthew Taylor, 70pp, paperback, VSO/ITDG, ISBN 185339214 6

Participatory Forestry – The process of change in India and Nepal by Mary Hobley, 360pp, paperback, VSO/ODI, ISBN 0 85003 204 0

Using Technical Skills in Community Development – An analysis of VSO's experience by Jonathan Dawson, ed Mog Ball, 55pp, paperback, VSO/ITP, ISBN 1 85339 078 X

Water Supplies for Rural Communities by Colin and Mog Ball, 56pp, paperback, VSO/ITP, ISBN 1 85339 112 3

For more information about VSO Books, contact:

VSO Books
317 Putney Bridge Road
London SW15 2PN
UK
Tel: (+44) (0) 181 780 2266
Fax: (+44) (0) 181 780 1326
e-mail: sbernau@vso.org.uk

Index